GUSCOTT · JAMIE ROBERTS · JJ W
McLAUCHLAN · KEITH WOOD · TAD
McBRIDE · RICHARD HILL · SEÁN O
LD DAVIES · JEREMY GUSCOTT · JA
GARETH EDWARDS · IAN McLAUCHL
ITOJE · WILLIE JOHN McBRIDE · R
JPR WILLIAMS · GERALD DAVIES ·
S BARRY JOHN · GARETH EDWARDS
URLONG · MARO ITOJE · WILLIE JO
N · MERVYN DAVIES · JPR WILLIAM
IE ROBERTS · JJ WILLIAMS · BARRY
KEITH WOOD · URLONG
D HILL · SEÁN O BRIEN · MERVYN I
Y GUSCOTT · JAMIE ROBERTS · JJ W
McLAUCHLAN · KEITH WOOD · TAD
McBRIDE · RICHARD HILL · SEÁN O
LD DAVIES · JEREMY GUSCOTT · JAI
GARETH EDWARDS · IAN McLAUCHL
ITOJE · WILLIE JOHN McBRIDE · R
JPR WILLIAMS · GERALD DAVIES ·
S BARRY JOHN · GARETH EDWARDS
URLONG · MARO ITOJE · WILLIE JO

The
IMMORTALS
of British & Irish Rugby

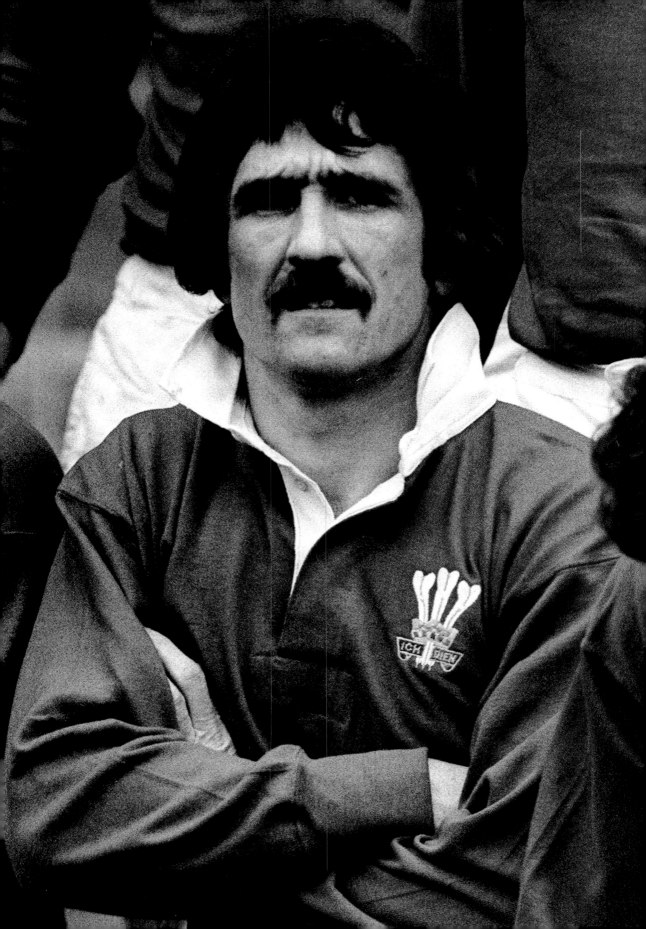

The
IMMORTALS
of British & Irish Rugby

John Westerby

A Gelding Street Press book
An imprint of Rockpool Publishing

PO Box 252
Summer Hill
NSW 2130 Australia

geldingstreetpress.com

ISBN: 9781922662064

Published in 2024 by Rockpool Publishing

Design and typesetting by Christine Armstrong, Rockpool Publishing
Publisher: Luke West, Rockpool Publishing
Edited by Brooke Halliwell

A catalogue record for this
book is available from the
National Library of Australia

Printed and bound in China
10 9 8 7 6 5 4 3 2 1

DEDICATION

For any player selected for the British & Irish
Lions. All Lions are worthy of recognition – those who
feature in this book are simply the best of the best.

CONTENTS

Mervyn Davies, a remarkably skilful loose forward for Wales and the Lions, who changed the way the No8 position was seen

INTRODUCTION

There are few conversations that animate followers of British and Irish rugby union quite as much as picking their Lions team. Even though the Lions go on tour only once every four years, each season, during and after the Six Nations championship, supporters in the pubs and rugby clubs of England, Ireland, Scotland and Wales will engage in heated debates over which 15 players should make up a composite team from their four nations. And then every fourth year, those discussions are energised further still, because such a team is actually going to exist. The head coach of the British & Irish Lions will be doing exactly the same thing as those fans in the pubs, but for real, choosing the best players from England, Ireland, Scotland and Wales, to come together as one for a tour to New Zealand, South Africa or Australia.

Those players will just have spent their winter knocking lumps out of each other; soon they will be together in the same changing room, wearing the same red shirts and, with only a few weeks preparation, will be asked to compete alongside players they have never played with before. They may not even know some of their Lions teammates at the start of the tour, but by the end, particularly if the tour is successful, they will have forged bonds to last a lifetime.

In many ways, this idea of an eclectic touring team is a wonderfully old-fashioned construct, and many feared that the sport's professional era, from the mid-1990s onwards, would sound a death knell for the Lions. In fact, as the Sea of Red supporters adorning Lions tours illustrates so vividly, the concept is alive and kicking, as big and bright as ever, all the more special because of its long and varied history. Along with winning the World Cup, representing the British & Irish Lions remains the ultimate honour available to a player from those four nations. There really is nothing else quite like the Lions.

Picking a team of Immortals who have worn the red shirt, then, elevates the pub conversation to a whole different level. To be considered in this company, a player must be one of the rarefied breed

The British & Irish Lions, the pick of players from England, Ireland, Scotland and Wales, line up before facing Australia in the first Test in Brisbane in 2013

who have not only been chosen for the Lions, but have dazzled in the red shirt when the opportunity has come their way, writing themselves into Lions history. They stand a much stronger chance of being picked for our team if they have contributed significantly to a successful Test series for the Lions: those players whose feats resonate down the ages, whose names become indelibly associated with the Lions, are most likely to be those who have played in a team that has conquered the All Blacks, the Springboks or the Wallabies. Winning a series with the Lions really is a step towards becoming an Immortal of your sport.

Over the coming chapters, we will select a starting line-up of Immortals in the traditional order, from full back through to scrum half in the backs, from loosehead prop through to No8 in the forwards, followed by a bench of eight replacements from those who narrowly missed out. Some selection criteria have been laid down: the candidates must have played in more than one Lions Test series. This rules out a few luminaries who have shone on their only trip with the Lions, the likes of David Duckham in New Zealand in 1971, Mike Teague, man of the series in Australia in 1989, George North and Alex Corbisiero against the Wallabies in 2013. Their deeds in helping to win those series are etched in Lions folklore. But to be considered a true Immortal for present purposes, there is a requirement to have performed across more than one series.

Historical limits have also been set. Although the Lions have been touring since 1888, the choices made have been restricted mainly to the last 60 years, to the mid-1960s, with only the odd sortie a little further back. Choosing a team from candidates who span different eras inevitably creates its own selectorial challenges. The game has inevitably changed and such choices can only ever be subjective, but that's what selection and pub conversations are about. Comparing the performances of, say, Barry John in the early 1970s and Johnny Sexton more recently, two undeniably masterful fly halves, is never going to be an exact science, but the impact they had on the game at large as well as their performances in those successful series have been taken into account.

One big change that had to be weighed into consideration was the vast improvements that have been made in defence in the professional era. In comparison with the modern game, watching footage from previous generations is often to see, in relative terms, disorganised defence and half-hearted tackling from some players (okay, yes, mainly the backs). It was only once the game turned professional in 1995 and the influence of rugby league began to be felt that rugby union began to take defence seriously. Indeed, the Lions' triumph in South Africa in 1997 was built in part on the defensive improvements brought by a raft of players recently returned to the 15-man code from rugby league. But there were other factors that worked against attacking players in previous generations, such as the quality of the pitches and a ball that could become heavier in wet conditions.

As with any team selection, there are a couple of players in the Immortals line-up who effectively picked themselves. Most of the participants in our pub conversation would, I think, concur with the choices of JPR Williams at full back and Gareth Edwards at scrum half. Every other choice is probably more contentious, but a couple of selections were particularly tricky to make. There have been plenty of second-row forwards who have been genuine Lions greats, some of them bringing immense leadership qualities, too. Martin Johnson is one such player, the tough-as-teak captain of the Lions in South Africa in 1997 and Australia four years later, as well as leading England to the World Cup. To some, he is the embodiment of the Lions spirit.

But there was also another tough-as-teak captain of the Lions to consider, by the name of Willie John McBride. He went on five tours, including the epic adventures of 1971 in New Zealand and as captain of the 'Invincibles' in South Africa in 1974. Those tours revived the Lions as a concept after a long barren run and raised the global profile of the game. To my mind, it was Johnson *or* McBride, not both. One of them must pack down alongside Maro Itoje, whose all-round brilliance brings a different dynamic to the second-row pairing, winning selection for his remarkable performances in New Zealand in 2017 and South Africa in 2021. McBride is the natural captain of the Immortals, so Johnson misses out.

The choice of an inside centre was also a thorny issue. John Dawes? Scott Gibbs? Jamie Roberts? Dawes was part of that backline for the ages that beat the All Blacks in 1971, Gibbs was sensational in South Africa in 1997. Jonathan Davies played a couple of games at No12

in the 2013 series in Australia, appearing at outside centre the rest of the time in that series and 2017, but he has been nudged out at No13 by Jeremy Guscott. In the end, Roberts got the nod for his outstanding efforts in 2009, in particular, and also in the series-clinching win in 2013. I felt that he was a similarly physical force in defence to Gibbs, if slightly less so, but a greater force in attack. Others may disagree and they are thoroughly welcome to do so.

Our final 15 break down on geographical lines as follows: seven from Wales, four from Ireland, three from England and one from Scotland (but two of the replacements are Scots). The strong Welsh influence merely reflects the preponderance of players from their golden generation in those classic Lions teams of the early 1970s. As an aside, it was interesting to note that four of the Immortals – Gerald Davies, Barry John, Gareth Edwards and Mervyn Davies – were the sons of Welsh miners and another three – McBride, Tadhg Furlong and Seán O'Brien – have come from Irish farming families. If you were to combine those two gene pools, you really would have some useful rugby players.

Jeremy Guscott, the Lions' princely centre, celebrates after his drop-goal had clinched the series-winning victory over South Africa in Durban in 1997

The opportunity to perform for the British & Irish Lions is a narrow window in itself: a few weeks every four years, with only three Tests, and if injury strikes at the wrong time, the chance can be gone. There are great players from England, Ireland, Scotland and Wales who have never had the chance to shine for the Lions; good form and fortune with injuries are essential. But for those who make it on tour, who throw themselves wholeheartedly into the fray with a squad drawn from four rival nations, the chance to become Lions legends awaits.

The 15 players profiled here have all taken their chances and fully deserve to be seen as the Immortals of British & Irish rugby.

JPR Williams, the supreme Wales full back, one of the first names on the team sheet in any all-time Lions line-up

JPR Williams

Name	JPR Williams
Birthdate	2 March 1949 (died 8 January 2024)
Birthplace	Bridgend
Country	Wales (55 caps)
Position	Full back – No15
Lions caps	8

Strong and brave, with the skills of a back and the mentality of a forward, JPR Williams was a rock at full back for Wales and the Lions in the 1970s.

The phrase 'Test match animal' has become indelibly associated with the British & Irish Lions, popularised by Ian McGeechan as an indicator of the qualities required in a player to thrive on the biggest sporting stages, against the toughest of opponents, in the most challenging situations. As a player on two Lions tours in the 1970s, then a head coach on four more, McGeechan knows better than anyone what makes a successful Lion.

Those qualities were unquestionably present in abundance in JPR Williams, one of the greatest full backs the game has seen, and another Lions coach recognised animal tendencies that he characterised, memorably, in a different way. Carwyn James was the coach for the tour to New Zealand in 1971, for which he picked Williams when the Wales full back was only 22. He then watched him play an all-action role in a rousing series victory, the only one the Lions have achieved against the All Blacks to date.

'Like a forest animal, he was blessed with a sixth sense for the presence of danger, an element which he often sought and loved,' James later wrote. 'Fearless. Uncompromising. The competitor of competitors.'

The way in which Williams sensed and embraced danger shaped his

If he had not opted for rugby and medicine, professional tennis might have been a viable career option for JPR Williams

facets of his game, in defence and attack, along with his distinctive appearance – socks rolled down, hair flowing, rockstar sideburns – made him one of the most watchable players ever to have represented the British & Irish Lions.

He played in an era that was hugely successful both for Wales and the Lions; no coincidence there, as Williams was one of a number of gifted players behind those successes that remain household names in Wales and beyond. Over the course of his international career, which ran from 1969 to 1981, Wales won the Five Nations title six times, three of which came with the fabled grand slam. Eleven times he played against England, the fixture that stirs a Welshman more than any other, and, remarkably, he finished on the winning side 11 times.

Members of that Wales team of the early 1970s formed the backbone of the Lions squads that achieved historic victories in New Zealand in 1971 and South Africa three years later, two of the greatest Lions tours. Williams would undoubtedly have been selected to tour New Zealand again in 1977 had he not, in those amateur days, opted to remain at home to

game in both defence and attack. As the last line of defence, often standing alone as the only obstacle between an onrushing opponent and the tryline, he was resolutely physical and courageous. With the ball in hand, he was a pioneer in launching thrilling counterattacks from deep in his own half, a strategy always laced with risk, but one offering vast potential rewards. Together, the mastery of these twin

focus on his medical career on his path to becoming a surgeon.

But he continued excelling for Wales, exhibiting those defining qualities of foursquare solidity in defence and eye-catching dash in attack. He loved the game so much that, once his career at the highest level was over, he kept playing club rugby, first for Bridgend, then eventually at a much lower level for Tondu, turning out for their third team into his fifties. By that time, the attacking élan was not so much in evidence and he had shifted to play at flanker, still showing that same relish for danger and for the physical side of the game.

Born in Bridgend on 2 March 1949 – he missed out on a St David's Day arrival by a few hours – he was the eldest of four boys and both his parents were doctors. His mother, Margaret, was actually English, coming from Rochdale, but his father, Peter, was the son of a miner and grew up in Pontypridd with a love for rugby and tennis. Along with his brothers, the young JPR grew up dreaming of playing rugby in the blue and white of Bridgend, but they also showed a real flair for tennis. All four brothers, in fact, played junior rugby for Bridgend

The paths he was following in rugby and tennis would soon cross again and force a decision on his future sporting direction.

and all four would go on to become Welsh junior tennis champions. Not a bad record for one family.

Tennis remained a major part of Williams' life throughout his teenage years to the extent that turning professional was a viable career option for him. He won the British boys' title at Wimbledon in 1966, beating David Lloyd, who would go on to play Davis Cup for Great Britain. Two years later, he was playing in a tournament at Bournemouth – the first professional event after tennis had entered its 'open' era – and, after winning his qualifying match, he earned himself a prize of £20 and felt the need to check that accepting the money did not compromise his amateur status in rugby.

In the next round of that tournament, he was beaten in straight sets by Bob Howe, a former quarter-finalist at the Australian Open. To ease his disappointment, he was driven by his father back from Bournemouth to play for Bridgend against Newport, arriving back in the nick of time for an evening kick-off. He had an outstanding game, pulling off two brilliant tackles on Stuart Watkins, the Wales winger at the time, and his performance went some way towards him gaining selection, aged 19, for the national team's development tour to Argentina that summer.

The paths he was following in rugby and tennis would soon cross again and force a decision on his future sporting direction. The pivotal moment came while he was competing in the British Under 21 championships in Manchester and had reached the quarter-finals, but there was a clash with a training session Wales had organised in preparation for that development tour to Argentina. Williams withdrew from the tennis tournament, travelled to Argentina in the summer and then made his international debut for Wales, still only 19, against Scotland at Murrayfield in the Five Nations championship the following season.

The decision had been made, influenced in part by his desire to study at one of London's prestigious medical schools, where a talent for rugby could be a considerable help in securing a place: he would be an amateur rugby player and medical professional, rather than attempting to forge a career in tennis. 'I could have looked to become a tennis professional,' he said. 'But my father said to me: "Sport is for enjoyment, not for money. You get a proper job". I haven't regretted it at all. My father was right, in my opinion. You do take sport seriously, but it's not the end of the world.'

After that international debut at Murrayfield, Williams played in every match of the 1969 Five Nations, in which Wales remained unbeaten, but were denied the grand slam by a draw in Paris. They completed the tournament with a thumping 30–9 victory over England in Cardiff, the first of that incredible record of 11 victories against Wales' great rivals. The following year, at Twickenham, he scored his first international try, timing his burst into the line to perfection as Chico Hopkins, the scrum half, went blind from a scrum and Williams crashed through a tackle to score.

At this stage, he was still known as plain old John Williams, and that would remain the case until another player by the same name was picked on the wing for Wales

Williams dives over to score his first international try, against England at Twickenham. He never lost a match against England

in 1973. When John Williams the winger was involved in a passage of play with John Williams the full back, it became confusing for television commentators and their audience, so the speedy bloke on the wing became JJ and the hairy full back became JPR, three initials – for John Peter Rhys – that became so familiar to a sporting audience that the surname became all but redundant. He was still John to his family, but to the rest of the world he was JPR.

The two Williamses combined to telling effect in what was perhaps JPR's finest performance against England, in the grand slam season of 1976, when he scored two memorable tries. The full back always seemed to raise his game on

Wales' visits to Twickenham and this year Wales opened their Five Nations with a 21–9 win in south-west London. No surprise, perhaps, that he settled so happily in London in the early stages of his medical career, first at St Mary's Hospital Medical School, then playing for London Welsh from 1968 to 1976, when he returned to Bridgend.

The first of those two tries at Twickenham came as the ball was swept swiftly from right to left, reaching JJ Williams on the wing, and he flipped a pass back inside to his namesake, who powerfully brushed aside two tackles to score. The second try showcased his searing acceleration, running onto an inside pass from Phil Bennett, then changing direction and racing away as English tacklers attempted to cling onto him from either side. He was quite a sight in full flow and his muscular athleticism made him a nightmare for defenders to bring down.

His early promise on the international stage, along with Wales' dominant displays, had earned Williams his first Lions call-up for the tour to New Zealand in 1971. At that point, he had played 16 times for his country and over the three Five Nations championships he had played in, Wales had been beaten only once. After they had won the title in 1969, though, Wales had been on tour to New Zealand and Australia. Although they beat the Wallabies narrowly in Sydney, they were badly beaten twice by the All Blacks, losing 19–0 in Christchurch and 33–12 in Auckland. 'That beating was very important for the 1971 Lions,' Williams later said. 'We all learned from losing to the All Blacks at a time when we thought we were pretty good.'

The Welsh contingent in that Lions squad knew just how good they would have to be if they were to win a series in New Zealand for the first time. And they took the series by storm, starting with a 9–3 win in Dunedin, losing the second Test

Williams in full flow for London Welsh, the club he joined when he moved to pursue medical studies at St Mary's Hospital Medical School

in Christchurch, but surging back to win 13–3 in Wellington, establishing a 2–1 lead in the series with the final Test in Auckland to come.

In a series in which their backs were outstanding, Williams' counterattacking from full back and his solidity under the high ball had been a feature of the Lions' progress. But in the final Test, he revealed an aspect of his game that had hitherto remained fairly well hidden. Kicking is always a part of the full back's skillset, but Williams, instinctively, had always preferred to run. On the bus on the way to that final Test in Auckland, Williams sought to amuse his nervous teammates. 'I thought I'd try to make them all laugh, I told them I'd drop a goal,' he said. 'No one believed me.' Bob Hiller, his fellow full back, bet him that he wouldn't.

The decisive Test, unsurprisingly, was a tense, closely fought affair, with the scores level at 11–11 in the 54th minute when the ball, with a Lions attack going nowhere, came to Williams 45 metres out. He knew instantly what he wanted to do, gave the ball an almighty wallop, and sent it soaring through the posts to the disbelief of both the All Blacks and his teammates. In celebration, he raised his arm over to the Lions bench, just to let Hiller know he would be along later to collect his winnings.

It would prove to be the winning kick. The All Blacks equalised with a penalty to draw the match 14–14, but the Lions had won the series. It would also prove to be the only drop-goal that Williams would kick in the entirety of his international career. Talk about picking your moment.

That natural inclination to run the ball was, undoubtedly, due in part to an unquenchably adventurous streak of Williams' character. But it owed something, too, to a change in the game's laws that dovetailed neatly with his career, almost uncanny in its timing. In September 1968, in an attempt to limit the amount of kicking to touch, the laws were altered so that the ball could only be kicked out on the full from inside the player's own 22-metre line. If it went directly into touch from outside the 22, the resultant lineout would be from where the ball was kicked, rather than where it crossed into touch.

The aim was to encourage more running from deep and this suited Williams just nicely. Once they had played a few times together, the understanding he developed with the likes of Gerald Davies and JJ Williams, his back-three colleagues for Wales and the Lions, was the source of countless attacks from deep. They knew that when the ball was kicked in the general direction of JPR, a counterattack was on the cards and they would hare after him in support.

This understanding between full back and winger was demonstrated beautifully in the third Test of the Lions' tour to South Africa in 1974. The Lions had won the first Test

Another successful visit to Twickenham for Williams, this time in 1978 on the way to clinching Wales' third Five Nations grand slam in the 1970s

on a mudbath of a pitch in Cape Town, then produced a polished performance to go 2–0 up in the series in Pretoria. They travelled to Port Elizabeth knowing they could clinch a famous series victory.

The Springboks came intent on intimidating their opponents, with a huge first-half punch-up erupting. The Lions not only stood up to the physical onslaught, they outplayed the Springboks with some brilliant rugby, the opening try seeing the Williams duo in perfect synchronicity. First JJ made ground on the outside, passing inside to JPR, who then returned the favour by taking the outside line, flipping a pass back inside,

where JJ was waiting to score the opening try. It was then JPR who started the counterattack that led to JJ's second try, gathering his own kick ahead, and the Lions were on their way to one of their greatest victories, having demonstrated consummate skill, but also an extraordinary toughness.

Those same qualities were ever evident in the play of JPR Williams. Time and again in that series in South Africa, he was assailed by swarms of his opponents, who knew all too well his value to the Lions and the effect it would have if he were cowed. Williams never took a backward step. 'He was just one of those devastating players that never seemed to get hurt,' said Ian Kirkpatrick, a Springboks selector in 1974.

As the last line of defence, the barrier of physical courage and sheer strength that Williams presented to the opposition was never better illustrated than in one famed try-saving tackle he executed on Jean-François Gourdon, the France right winger. In the Five Nations clash in Cardiff in 1976, Gourdon ran onto a pass from Jean-Claude Skrela at breakneck speed, only 20 metres out, a seemingly unstoppable object with a clear path to the line. A try looked an absolute certainty until JPR, the immovable object, suddenly appeared, barging Gourdon unceremoniously into touch. It would be classed as an illegal tackle today, but back then it was rapturously received by the Cardiff crowd.

It was often said that he tackled like a flanker and when Wales were beset by injuries on their tour to Australia in 1978, Williams actually played a Test at openside, wearing No7. Nice preparation for those later days with Tondu third team.

There is no shortage of tales of JPR's bloody-minded bravery. Playing for Bridgend against the touring All Blacks in 1978, he was the victim of a brutally cynical stamp on the side of his face from John Ashworth, the

'Bloody typical, isn't it? The car's a write-off, the tanker's a write-off. But JPR comes out of it in one piece.'
— *Gareth Edwards*

All Blacks prop. Williams' cheek was ripped open, a hideous sight, and he was forced to leave the field. Astonishingly, 15 minutes later, a huge cheer erupted among the crowd as Williams was returning to the field. His cheek had been sewn back together, with the small matter of 30 stitches, lovingly applied by the Bridgend team doctor, who just happened to be his father.

It was Gareth Edwards who best summed up his teammate's ability apparently to emerge from any manner of physical scrape after Williams had crashed his car into a lorry. 'Bloody typical, isn't it?' Edwards said. 'The car's a write-off, the tanker's a write-off. But JPR comes out of it in one piece.'

Gerald Davies was one of a host of London Welsh players in the late 1960s and early 1970s who went on to play for the Lions

GERALD DAVIES

Name	Gerald Davies
Birthdate	7 February 1945
Birthplace	Llansaint
Country	Wales (46 caps)
Position	Right wing – No14
Lions caps	5

Quick and graceful, Gerald Davies was a beautifully balanced runner and instinctive finisher, requiring little time or space to find his way to the tryline.

It still prompts a smile to think that Gerald Davies was, in the first instance, a notably reluctant winger. A centre by preference in his earlier days, he won his first 11 caps for Wales wearing No12, relishing the opportunity to get his hands on the ball as often as possible, to stay in the thick of the action, to shape the game rather than wait for it. His first Test cap for the Lions, against South Africa in 1968, came in midfield, too. And when he was asked by Clive Rowlands, the Wales coach, to move to the wing amid an injury crisis in 1969? 'At the time,' Davies said, 'I saw it as a demotion.'

At 5ft 9in and 11st 9lb, it might have been that the steadily increasing physical nature of the game in the 1970s saw him naturally shift out from the centre to a wider position anyway. But once he was on the right wing, Davies displayed such a finely polished set of skills that he immediately looked to the manner born. In the first five matches he started on the wing for Wales, he scored six tries. Throughout their golden era in the 1970s, he adorned the Welsh attack, his pace, balance, nimble footwork and eye for the corner making decisive contributions on a regular basis.

He might not have handled the ball as many times as he would have done in the centre, but the extra space he had in the wider

Davies took a break from rugby in 1970 to focus on his education, following a teaching degree at Loughborough with English literature studies at Cambridge

channels gave him a canvas to express his gifts and he did not need many opportunities. It was all done with a dash of style, too, his collar turned up, hair and moustache immaculately trimmed, even amid the rough and tumble of a Test match. 'He was a magical man to have in your team because he could turn a game with one run,' said John Dawes, who played inside him at centre for Wales and the Lions. 'He could do things that other players could only dream about.'

Having started out at Llanelli, ten miles from his home village of Llansaint, he was at university at Loughborough and playing for Cardiff by the time he made his Wales debut, against Australia at the Arms Park. Although they slipped to a narrow defeat, it was an auspicious day for Wales,

because also making his debut that day at fly half was Barry John, two of the future stars of the golden generation, both still only 21, taking their first steps together on the international stage.

Davies would go on to enjoy unprecedented success over the course of his Wales career, winning five Five Nations titles (plus another two where they finished joint top), including three grand slams. In those early days, though, the good times had not yet begun to roll, and the first four matches he played for his country all ended in defeat, the loss to Australia followed by Five Nations setbacks against Scotland, Ireland and France. To avert a complete washout, in their final game they needed to beat an England side who had eyes on a potential title.

That contest in Cardiff would come to be known as the Keith Jarrett match after the 18-year-old centre Wales selected out of position at full back for his international debut. Jarrett responded with an extraordinary performance, streaking away for a spectacular try and kicking seven goals. But this was also the day that Davies, playing in the centre, scored his first two international tries, both of them beauties. The first came from a wonderful counterattack as John Lloyd, the prop, gathered the loose ball in his own half and passed to Davies, who released Dewi Bebb down the left wing. Bebb made good ground down the left and, as he was tackled by Roger Hosen, the England full back, he looked up to find Davies supporting him, and Davies sprinted the last 30 metres to score.

For his second try, he took a pass in midfield from John Taylor, the flanker, 25 metres out. There was still much to do, but Davies dipped his shoulder, stepped off his left foot to swerve outside Rod Webb, the England left wing, and suddenly a path to the right-hand corner appeared before him. He accelerated away and a pursuing posse of English defenders did not

'He was a magical man to have in your team because he could turn a game with one run.'
– *John Dawes*

come close to laying a hand on him. Nobody knew it at the time, but that try showcased the skills that would go on to make him one of the world's greatest wingers. For the time being, Wales had salvaged their season with a 34–21 win over the old enemy and Davies was off the mark in international rugby.

Still only 23, he was chosen the following year to tour South Africa with the British & Irish Lions. It was an honour, of course, but all the more special that the trip was to face the Springboks. As a 10-year-old boy, Davies had become entranced by the Lions' visit to South Africa in 1955 by making regular visits to the cinema in Llanelli to watch footage of the tour on *Pathé News*. 'Rugby to me was going to Stradey Park [Llanelli's home ground], standing on the Tanner Bank and shivering in the cold,' he said. 'Watching those films, I saw rugby teams playing in sunlight, below blue skies with palm trees visible. Watching those Lions struck a great chord of adventure.'

The 1968 tour was not a roaring success, either for Davies or the Lions, who drew the second Test with the Springboks, but lost the other three. He had made the Test team for the third match of the series, starting at inside centre in the 11–6 defeat in Cape Town, but like the squad as a whole, Davies was dogged by injuries, first an ankle problem that he picked up early in the tour and struggled to shake off, then a dislocated elbow in the tour match against Free State that brought his tour to a premature end.

Yet that tour had served a vital purpose in terms of sowing seeds for future success. Davies, Barry John, Gareth Edwards and John Taylor all had their first experiences of a Lions tour, none was older than 23 in South Africa, and by the time they toured New Zealand with the Lions three years later, the experience would stand them in good stead.

After a successful Five Nations in 1969, further formative experiences would follow when Wales played two Tests in New Zealand in 1969, losing both Tests heavily. It was before the second of those matches that Rowlands, needing to reshuffle his three-quarter line because of an injury to Stuart Watkins, came up with the idea of moving Davies from the centre to take Watkins' place. Davies had to be persuaded, but eventually he agreed.

He would play on the wing the following week, too, against Australia at the Sydney Cricket Ground, where Wales came back from 8–0 down in muddy conditions to secure a much-needed 19–16 win. This was where Davies first really looked the part as an international winger, taking a pass from Jarrett at pace 40 yards out on his wing, then jinking beautifully inside Arthur McGill, the Wallabies' full back, to score a crucial try. It was a sign of things to come. The way in which Davies was able to shift direction subtly and late, off either foot, while still travelling at full speed, made him desperately difficult for defenders to stop, and those twinkletoed steps would become his trademark. There was an almost balletic quality to his footwork, such was his supreme balance.

He had learned to sidestep, he said, growing up watching Carwyn James play fly half for Llanelli, and went on to practise the manoeuvre endlessly on the training ground. As luck would have it, James would be the Lions' coach for the tour to New Zealand in 1971,

In typical fashion, Gerald Davies squeezes into the right corner for one of the two tries he scored in Wales' defeat of Ireland in Cardiff in 1971

and he would reap the benefits of all that Davies had learned.

Before he booked his place on another Lions tour, though, Davies took a break. He opted not to play for Wales in the 1970 Five Nations to concentrate on completing his education. After first earning a teaching degree at Loughborough, he had gone on to study English literature at Cambridge, and feared that too much rugby, with the long journeys to and from Cardiff to prepare for internationals, would adversely affect his studies.

The importance of education had been drilled into him by his father, Tudor, a coal miner, who had wanted his son to study hard to avoid following him down the

pit. He loved rugby and had played the game himself, but he was keen that education, rather than rugby, was his son's overriding priority. The message was heeded and, although he missed a shared Five Nations title in 1970, Gerald was back on the wing for Wales at the start of the tournament the following season.

And 1971 would turn out to be quite some year. Far from suffering from his time away from playing at the highest level, he was coming back to the game fresh, having not only furthered his education, but also, as he turned 26 during the Five Nations, with the lessons learned from those tours to South Africa and New Zealand in his locker.

His first game back in the red shirt was in Cardiff against England,

In the colours of London Welsh, Davies struck up a harmonious understanding with JPR Williams, which they further developed with Wales and the Lions

the first time he had played on the wing for his country in front of his home crowd. It did not take long for them to be shown the wisdom of his conversion, as he scored two tries in a thumping 22–6 victory. His first was produced by slick handling among the Welsh backs, Davies keeping his width on the wing, then taking a sweetly timed pass from John Dawes 25 metres out and outsprinting the English cover to dive in the corner. The second came after Peter Rossborough, the England full back, had dropped a towering kick from Edwards, which was quickly regathered by Arthur Lewis and Dawes once again put Davies away.

The next game was a famously tight contest at Murrayfield that swung back and forth until Scotland were leading 18–14 with three minutes left, the Edinburgh crowd approaching fever pitch. From clean lineout ball on the left, palmed down by Delme Thomas, Wales launched a determined late attack, moving the ball swiftly towards the right wing. Coming into the line, JPR Williams made an extra man and passed to Davies, who was still 20 metres from the line and 25 metres in from touch. There were two Scottish defenders in front of him, but he had the wide expanses of Murrayfield outside him to explore. He set off on an arcing route towards the corner, effectively taking the long way round, but backing his pace and momentum. He coasted outside Ian Smith, the full back, and Chris Rea, the centre, to cross in the corner and touch down five metres further in. Taylor, the flanker, kicked a nerveless left-footed conversion and Scottish hearts had been broken.

By now, Wales were building up a real head of steam, and they were much too strong for Ireland in Cardiff, winning 23–9 with another two tries from Davies, taking his tally to five in three games. The first of those, just before half-time, was a prime example of the majesty that Davies brought to wing play. As ever, the passing from his centres was excellent, this time Lewis drew his man and put the ball in Davies' path.

He was only a metre in from the touchline when he took the pass, 15 metres from the tryline, with a defender in front of him and reinforcements racing across. To look at a freeze-frame when he caught the ball, there was no obvious way through. But Davies, as ever, accelerated onto the ball, then stepped nimbly inside Barry Bresnihan, the Ireland centre, before veering outside Michael Hipwell to squeeze in at the corner.

It was all done in the blink of an eye, at breakneck speed, but Davies' try-scoring instincts and ability to make the most of minimal space were there for all to see.

The final game of the tournament was the only one in which Davies did not score, but Wales won in Paris for the first time in 14 years to clinch a memorable grand slam, ensuring their players would form the core of the British & Irish Lions squad selected to tour New Zealand that summer. With Dawes as captain and Carwyn James as coach, it was a Lions tour with a strong Welsh accent.

Six of the seven backs were Welsh for the first Test in Dunedin, although their only try in a gutsy 9–3 victory came from Ian McLauchlan, the Scottish prop. Although the All Blacks fought back to win the second match in Christchurch 22–12, the Lions' backs were beginning to show what they were capable of, not least in the first of two tries that Davies scored, a magnificent length-of-the-field counterattack. It was started by JPR Williams, fielding a kick from Sid Going near his own line, and the full back set off in search of adventure out of his 22 before he linked with Mike Gibson, who put Davies away near the halfway line. The timing of Davies' run was perfect, the acceleration as he ran onto the pass leaving the New Zealand defence for dead. The All Blacks now knew that this was a Lions team capable of scoring tries from anywhere.

Between the second and third Tests, Davies enjoyed a field day against Hawke's Bay, scoring four tries as the Lions, ever more cohesive as the tour wore on, continued to play some scintillating rugby. One step off his right foot left the Hawke's Bay full back flat on his back as Davies crossed the line, while he burst onto a bouncing kick from Gibson to score again.

The wind was now in the sails of the touring team and they carried their momentum into the third Test at Wellington, storming into a 13–0 lead by half-time. Davies was on the scoresheet again, a short-range score, by his standards, after Edwards had broken to the blindside of a ruck. There was no way back for New Zealand, the Lions won 13–3 and were 2–1 up with just the final Test to come. A momentous 14–14 draw in Auckland then ensured that they would ink their names in the history books as the first – and, to date, the only – Lions side to win a series in New Zealand. There was a rapturous

reception when they arrived back at Heathrow Airport. 'There were extraordinary scenes of cheering and singing in a way I imagine the Beatles experienced,' Davies said. 'It was a gloriously unforgettable moment.'

So Davies' status as a Lions legend was secure, but the next time the chance came to tour, to South Africa in 1974, he turned down the opportunity. In part, this was because he had a new job as a teacher and a young family. It was also because of his feelings about the apartheid regime, which he had experienced on the Lions tour of 1968, during which he had wanted to meet a friend from Loughborough University, who was Cape Coloured, and had not been allowed to admit him to the team hotel. 'It was between myself and my conscience and I never regretted that decision,' Davies said. Thirty-five years later, there was some nice symbolism when Davies was chosen as manager of the 2009 Lions tour to South Africa, the days of apartheid long since in the past.

He went on to enjoy plenty more success for Wales, achieving two more grand slams in 1976 and 1978, cementing the place of that 1970s vintage in the nation's

Davies was tour manager for the Lions on their 2009 trip to South Africa, pictured here with Ian McGeechan (left), the coach, and Paul O'Connell (centre), the captain

collective consciousness. It was not just their success, it was the way they went about their rugby, too, and Davies played a huge part in that. One of the tries often picked out as an example of that team's capabilities came against Scotland at Murrayfield in the 1977 Five Nations. This time Davies was not the scorer, featuring earlier in the move, taking Wales out of their own 22 with two outrageous sidesteps, followed by a hand-off worthy of someone twice his size. The move swept downfield and was finished brilliantly by Phil Bennett. The same year, he produced two piercing steps off his right foot and a lovely pass to send Clive Burgess over the line. In one of the game's finest teams, Davies

scored 20 tries in 46 Tests, but was so much more than just a finisher.

His final Test appearances came on tour to Australia in 1978. There were two Tests, he captained Wales in the second of them and, wouldn't you know, he scored in both. In the second Test, he took a pass 10 metres from the line from JPR Williams – playing at flanker that day – and, with precious little room, dived neatly into the corner, one more fabulous finish. It was a fitting way to sign off for a player who was so evidently a winger to his bootstraps, even if he would have preferred to remain as a centre.

Jeremy Guscott playing for the Lions on the 1993 tour to New Zealand, the second of his three Lions trips

JEREMY GUSCOTT

Name	Jeremy Guscott
Birthdate	7 July 1965
Birthplace	Bath
Country	England (65 caps)
Position	Outside centre – No13
Lions caps	8

Guscott's attacking play came with a style that delighted the game's aesthetes, but he was a robust midfielder too, with a happy habit of seizing the big moments, which he demonstrated so capably in the red shirt of the Lions.

Not many journeys undertaken by British & Irish Lions legends have featured an important staging post in Bucharest. Rugby is a moderately popular sport in Romania, and the national team has featured in every World Cup bar one, but they have remained largely on the periphery of European rugby and have played against England only five times. But it was in Bucharest that Jeremy Guscott made a highly auspicious international debut in May 1989 in a 58–3 victory for England, scoring a hat-trick of tries.

It was a routine victory – England scored nine tries in all – and not the most demanding of international debuts, with plentiful ball supplied to the backs by a dominant pack. The timing, though, was significant. The game came shortly before the Lions were due to set off on tour to Australia and Ian McGeechan, the head coach, was on the lookout for a centre to replace Will Carling, the England captain, who had been forced to withdraw from the original squad to tour Australia due to a stress fracture to the shin.

The performance in Bucharest was not the game that ignited McGeechan's interest, because Guscott had been an influential

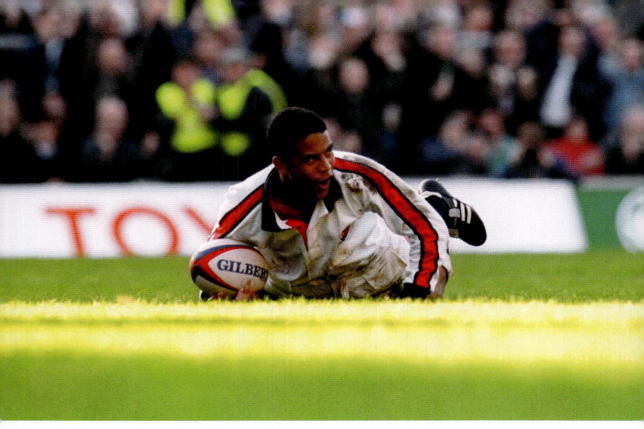

Guscott finishes with his customary style against France at Twickenham in 1995, helping England along the way to a third grand slam in five years

presence in the midfield for the Bath team that had just completed a league and cup double in the English club game, and the Lions coach had been watching with interest, but it was further evidence of the outside centre's striking talent. When McGeechan rang Jack Rowell, the Bath coach, to ask if he thought the 23-year-old had what it takes to thrive on grander stages, Rowell's answer convinced McGeechan that he had found the replacement centre he was seeking. Guscott's inexperience meant that there was an element of risk involved, but the Lions coach felt it was a gamble worth taking.

What he did not realise at the time was that he had found a player who would become a cornerstone of Lions Test teams for the next three tours. On two of those tours, Guscott made game-breaking contributions at decisive moments that helped the Lions to seal series wins. Very few players can lay claim to one of those, Guscott has two famous match-winning efforts to his name.

The first of those came on that first tour in 1989, when the Lions fought back from losing the first Test to win the series 2–1. In the dying moments of the second Test, Guscott conjured a brilliant try that ensured the series would go to the third

Test, collecting his own grubber kick and scoring by the posts. Eight years later in South Africa, he kicked the drop-goal that won the second Test for the Lions and with it the series. Cometh the moment, Guscott proved time and again that he had what it takes amid the pressures of a Lions series, that there was so much more to his game than the silky midfield running that saw him labelled as the 'prince of centres'.

That try against Australia was but one example of a prolific start to Guscott's international career. Some players take time to adjust to the step up from club to international rugby, but, coming from playing and training in such a strong environment at Bath, a team stuffed with internationals, Guscott took the move to the next level in his elegant stride. In his first nine international appearances, for England and the Lions, Guscott scored 10 tries.

His timing was fortunate, in a sense, because the England side he had broken into was a growing force under the captaincy of Carling and the coaching of Geoff Cooke, showing signs of emerging from a decade in the doldrums. By the time of the 1990 Five Nations, it had been 10 years since England had won more than half of their matches in the annual tournament. Guscott's first Five Nations, not entirely coincidentally, showed a marked improvement, with comprehensive victories in their first three matches and some exciting attacking rugby: England scored four tries to overcome Ireland at home, three more against France in Paris and another four at Twickenham against Wales.

The game against Ireland saw the blossoming of Guscott's centre pairing with Carling, which would become such a familiar feature over the next few years. Guscott was the older by five months, but Carling broke into international rugby a year earlier, becoming the youngest England captain at 22. They complemented each other well, Carling adept at running the straight lines and drawing defenders that would create the space his partner craved, but both had broad enough skillsets so that the roles could be reversed.

Against Ireland at Twickenham, Carling twice gave short, smart passes that sent Guscott purring away. The first of them saw Guscott make good ground before releasing a fine, long pass out to the right wing, where Rory Underwood careered away

To a local lad, who had been with the club since the age of seven, it was quite something to earn your stripes in the pre-eminent team of the era.

for a score. The second saw Carling occupy defenders and then slip a pass out to his centre partner, who picked a lovely line that saw him leave a crowd of green-shirted defenders trailing in his wake. This was thrilling rugby, of a type not seen from an England team for some time, and Guscott was quickly revealing himself to be a midfielder of rare athleticism, guile and grace.

The Five Nations that year came to a momentous climax when England travelled to Murrayfield to meet Scotland. Both sides had won their first three games, both were on the verge of a grand slam, a feat Scotland had not achieved for six years, England for 10. There was further evidence of that burgeoning centre partnership when Carling ran onto the ball at pace and released Guscott down the left, 30 yards out. Guscott was already flying, with Underwood in support outside him. Guscott did not need the support,

selling the cheekiest of dummies to Gavin Hastings, the Scotland full back, and outstripping the covering defence to dive over the line himself.

This was a day, though, when England were to come unstuck, as raw Scottish aggression prevailed amid a frenzied atmosphere. Guscott was forced off the field with a back injury in the second half and Scotland worked a superb try for Tony Stanger to clinch the grand slam for the home side. England, clearly, were building something special, and the lessons they learned would be put to good use over the next couple of years, but on this occasion they fell short.

It was a jolt to Guscott, too, because even at this early stage of his career, he had been used to winning. As a 19-year-old, somewhat slighter and with bigger hair, he had come off the bench to play on the wing in Bath's 1985 John Player Cup victory over London Welsh at Twickenham. This was one of a remarkable run of 10 cup victories in 12 years from the mid-1980s to the mid-1990s, the last years of the amateur game, to which they added six league titles, an unprecedented spell of dominance. To a local lad, who had been with the club since the age of seven, it was quite something to earn your stripes in the pre-eminent team of the era.

He had been born in Bath to Henry, a hospital porter who hailed from Jamaica, and an English mother, Sue, and went to Ralph Allen School, a comprehensive on the outskirts of the city, only a couple of miles from the Recreation Ground, Bath's unmistakable home ground. He was talented at a range of sports, football, cricket and judo among them, but Bath was a rugby city and that was where his affections lay. After leaving school, he began working as a bricklayer and then, briefly, a bus driver before going on to a job with British Gas that he could fit around his ever-increasing rugby commitments.

By the time he became a regular in the Bath first team, he was playing in the backline with England internationals such as Richard Hill, Stuart Barnes, Simon Halliday and Tony Swift, being given ample possession by a pack featuring Gareth Chilcott, Graham Dawe, Victor Ubogu, Nigel Redman, Jon Hall and Andy Robinson. Keeping that sort of company in his early years, perhaps it should have been no surprise that Guscott made the step up to international rugby so smoothly.

Guscott and John Bentley celebrate during the Lions' tour to South Africa in 1997, on which they both played starring roles

There was something else Guscott brought with him from Bath to England and, indeed, on to the Lions. Since the 1920s at Bath, the club had not worn the No13 shirt, the one that would generally be worn by an outside centre such as Guscott. Their centres would be No12 and No14, the right wing No15 and the full back No16. When

John Bentley, Scott Gibbs, Guscott, Alan Tait and Gregor Townsend, Lions' backs before the second Test against South Africa in 1997 in Durban, where they would famously clinch the series

he made the move to international rugby, with more than a hint of superstition, Guscott was keen to keep wearing the No12 shirt that had served him so well at club level and so his midfield partners, even though they were playing inside centre, would obligingly wear No13.

After the disappointment of the grand slam decider against Scotland in 1990, there was a fierce determination that England would go one better the following year. They did so in ruthless fashion, with a firmer focus on the power game made possible by a formidable pack

of forwards, built around the likes of Wade Dooley, Brian Moore and Dean Richards. English rugby seldom strays far from the conservative option when the chips are down and the 1991 Five Nations was a case in point: over the four games, England scored just five tries, seven fewer than the previous season, so there was less of a starring role for Guscott.

There would be greater entertainment in their later grand slams, in 1992 and 1995, blending the power of their forwards and the skill of their backs more effectively, but in 1990 the emphasis had been on getting the job done. Breaking the grand slam drought primed them nicely for a World Cup with a final on home soil later that year, but their style of play would again become a hot topic of debate. England had played their way into the final by once again utilising the might of their forward pack, especially in the memorably gutsy victories in the knockout stages over France and Scotland. Before the final against Australia at Twickenham, though, the question continued to be asked whether they should not be making more of such a talented bunch of backs, particularly the Carling and Guscott centre pairing, and the try-scoring verve of Underwood on the wing. Mischievously, David Campese, the Wallabies' agent provocateur, raised the issue publicly by suggesting that England were playing dull rugby and that they should open up a little more.

During the summer, England had toured Australia and, although they had lost the Test against the Wallabies, Guscott had contributed a fine try, making ground down the right wing before stepping inside Willie Ofahengaue to score. Some England players felt that similar inroads could be made again. In the final, England duly attempted to spread the ball more often, but had little luck against a well organised Australian defence. The Wallabies, ironically, scored a try through forward pressure, while England could manage only two penalty goals, and slumped to a 12–6 defeat.

Guscott had scored two lovely tries in a pool match against Italy, but finished the tournament feeling unfulfilled, a sensation that would recur in the three World Cups he played in, reaching the semi-final in 1995 and then bowing out of international rugby in 1999. 'I never played well in World Cups,' he said. 'It just never happened for me.'

The same could not be said, thankfully, for his times with the British & Irish Lions. With just that one international cap to his name in Bucharest, Guscott had arrived on the tour to Australia in 1989 as a firm outsider for a place in the Test team. But then the first Test in a three-match series was lost 30–12 in Sydney, conceding

He dropped the ball onto his left foot, threaded it delicately between the onrushing defenders and burst past them.

four tries to nil, and changes were needed for the second match in Brisbane. One more performance like that and the series was gone.

Despite his lack of exposure on the international stage, McGeechan plumped for Guscott in a revamped midfield. Scott Hastings and Guscott replaced Mike Hall and Brendan Mullin in the centre, and Rob Andrew came in for Craig Chalmers at fly half. With the series on the line, McGeechan knew that opting for inexperience was a bold move. 'Bringing Jerry in was a big call,' the coach said, 'definitely the biggest call I had to make on that tour.'

The game in Brisbane was dirty and the Lions gave at least as good as they got, the pack based around that uncompromisingly physical group of England forwards of the time. With only four minutes remaining, the Wallabies were 12–9 ahead, but Gavin Hastings edged the Lions in front with a well taken try. Still the nerves remained, at 13–12, until Guscott produced a moment of magic that confirmed the series would remain alive. Robert Jones launched a huge kick that was spilled by Campese, enabling Finlay Calder to surge deep into the Australian 22.

The ball was recycled swiftly and Andrew passed to Guscott, who had three Wallabies standing before him, with no apparent way through. Behind them, though, Guscott spotted space. He dropped the ball onto his left foot, threaded it delicately between the onrushing defenders and burst past them. The ball bounced up kindly and Guscott gathered to dive over the line. The series was still alive, the Lions would go on to win the final Test in Sydney and McGeechan's gamble on a Bath bricklayer with only one Test appearance behind him had paid off. The postscript was provided, knowingly, by Kevin Murphy, the Lions physio. 'That boy,' Murphy said, 'will never lay another brick again.'

Four years later, a squad led by Gavin Hastings were not able to become the second Lions side to win a series in New Zealand, but they succeeded in taking the series to the final Test. In an altogether tighter series, they scored only two tries in the three Tests, but Guscott was able to demonstrate the breadth of his skillset against powerful opponents. He played a key role in the try of the series, which came during the Lions' victory in the second Test in Wellington, timing his pass beautifully

That special feeling of winning a Lions series comes only to the fortunate few. Lawrence Dallaglio (left), Guscott and teammates soak up the moment in Durban in 1997

to send Underwood racing away for a brilliant score. But it was the quality of Guscott's defence that stood out for much of this demanding tour.

Such was the elegance of his attacking play that the toughness he showed in less glamorous aspects of the game was all too easily overlooked. He was strong, resolute in the tackle, and possessed the self-belief to assert himself against highly physical midfields. The importance of defence was growing quickly in the game and Guscott showed his mettle against the All Blacks in 1993. 'I went to New Zealand a bit of a namby-pamby runner, but was determined to show I could defend,' Guscott said. 'I think I did that, I was pleased with how I played.'

This was the tour, too, on which he struck up another of the game's great centre partnerships. After Carling had played inside him in the first Test defeat in Christchurch, for the second game Scott Gibbs was brought in to play alongside Guscott. Gibbs was a player whose defensive abilities could never be overlooked, a player standing 5ft 9in with shoulders almost as broad, who threw himself into tackles like a guided missile. The Welshman was a wonderful foil for Guscott, they quickly struck up an understanding in New Zealand, and the partnership would go from strength to strength against the Springboks four years later.

Jeremy Guscott had the pace, footwork and guile to keep opposing defenders guessing

Before the 1997 tour of South Africa, Guscott was not actually being picked as a first-choice centre by England. In the Five Nations that year, he came off the bench twice, but Carling had been replaced as captain by Phil de Glanville, another centre, and Rowell, now the England coach, wanted to retain Carling's services alongside the new captain. The Lions, however, were to be coached once again by McGeechan. From his two tours with Guscott, the Scot had no doubts.

He paired Gibbs and Guscott for all three Tests, but it would take only two to win the first series in South Africa since the fall of apartheid and the first since the game had turned professional. The first Test in Cape Town had been close and the Lions won 25–16, but the Springboks came back ferociously in the second Test in Durban. Battle as they might, the Lions were simply being overpowered, remaining in the contest only because South Africa's goal-kicking was woeful, in sharp contrast to the unerring boot of Neil Jenkins. The scoreboard read 15–15 and three minutes were remaining when the Lions forwards drove a maul towards the Springboks' line. Gregor Townsend, the fly half, then followed up with a burst

of his own, which left him buried beneath a pile of bodies and Guscott standing in the fly half's position.

In his junior rugby, Guscott had been a No10, but he was now almost 32, those days were long behind him and, for all his broad range of skills, his kicking game was seldom witnessed. But when Matt Dawson looked up and picked him out with a pass, 15 metres out and slightly to the left of the posts, he knew what he needed to do. He launched a drop-kick at goal, the ball rose high between the posts, and the Lions knew that the series was as good as won.

His sweet strike was one of the iconic moments in Lions history, the sort that prompts rugby fans to recall precisely where they were when they witnessed it. Guscott, as so often, was right at the centre of it all. 'The sense of elation when I looked up and saw the ball soar between the posts,' he said, 'is something that will stay with me forever.'

At his best, Jamie Roberts was desperately difficult to stop with ball in hand, as well as being robust in defence, an inside centre that a backline could be built around

JAMIE ROBERTS

Name	Jamie Roberts
Birthdate	8 November 1986
Birthplace	Newport
Country	Wales (94 caps)
Position	Inside centre – No12
Lions caps	3

Roberts announced his arrival on the global stage for the Lions against South Africa in 2009, showcasing the fearsome direct running style and uncompromising defence for which he would become known throughout the game.

Choosing a squad for a British & Irish Lions tour is like no other selection process. From the players representing the four home nations, the coach (or a committee in years gone by) is looking to pick players not only on the basis of their raw rugby ability or their recent performances for their country. He is picking players who he feels have the ability and the character to adapt to lining up alongside those they are not used to playing with. At the start of the tour, they may not even know each other. But in a few short weeks, they must come together as a squad, and eventually as a Test team, forging bonds on and off the field for the duration of that tour.

Ian McGeechan, who has chosen more Lions squads than anyone else, describes it as a search for chemistry, between individuals and among the group, and one of the greatest examples of finding this chemistry came on the 2009 tour to South Africa, when Jamie Roberts and Brian O'Driscoll struck up a centre partnership that looked as though it had been years in the making. Roberts, at 22, was relatively new to the international game with Wales. O'Driscoll was 30 and on his third

He would go on to establish himself as one of the best inside centres in the world.

Lions tour. As the head coach on that tour, McGeechan took great pleasure in seeing them emerge as a beautifully harmonious pairing, with complementary skillsets and rugby brains on a similar wavelength.

'Look at Brian O'Driscoll and Jamie Roberts on that tour,' McGeechan said. 'It gave them the chance to play as the best centre partnership in world rugby for one series. Because of their quality together, and the quality of people around them, they had an experience that was incredibly special. If you can get that chemistry right, that group of players, brought together for the first and only time, can do something they will never repeat.'

Although a gnawingly tight series was lost to South Africa 2–1, Roberts was named as man of the series, his hard, direct running the focal point for much of the Lions' best attacking play, his solidity in defence a bulwark against the ever-physical Springboks. His performances were all the more impressive because he had only been converted to

playing at No12 a year earlier, having emerged as a long-striding, hard-tackling full back for Cardiff Blues and made his international debut for Wales on the wing.

But he would go on to establish himself as one of the best inside centres in the world, one of the foundation stones of the powerful Wales team that enjoyed so much success during Warren Gatland's first spell in charge. With the potent ball-carrying from Roberts, all 6ft 5in and 17 stone of him, at the heart of all their playing style, Wales reached the semi-finals of the World Cup in New Zealand in 2011, knocked England out of their home tournament four years later and, during Roberts' time in the side, won three Six Nations titles. For the passionate and long-suffering Welsh fans, memories of the glory days of the 1970s were sparked back into life.

Gatland became head coach for the Lions' tour to Australia in 2013, too, and although a hamstring injury ruled Roberts out of the first two Tests, he was always going to be chosen for the Test side if fit. With the series level, he returned for the deciding Test in Sydney and played a prominent role in a crushing victory for the Lions, scoring the final try in a brilliant team performance. That was the Lions' first series win for 16 years, history had been made, and Roberts had been a key figure in two compelling Lions series.

All of which had been assiduously documented by Roberts' father, Norman, who has kept a meticulous archive of newspaper clippings, television recordings and memorabilia from his son's illustrious career. The love for rugby had been encouraged by Norman, a season ticket holder on the terraces at Newport for almost 30 years, who took his sons along to Rodney Parade from a young age. David was the elder son, 18 months Jamie's senior, although the younger sibling would outgrow his brother comprehensively in their teenage years.

The family moved from Newport to the northern suburbs of Cardiff when Jamie was young and, at the age of 6, he followed his brother to play junior rugby at CRICC, a largely Welsh-speaking local club. When the time came to look for more serious rugby, he joined some friends from his rugby-playing state school, Glantaf, who were playing at Rumney, a club in a tougher area of Cardiff, where Roberts learned

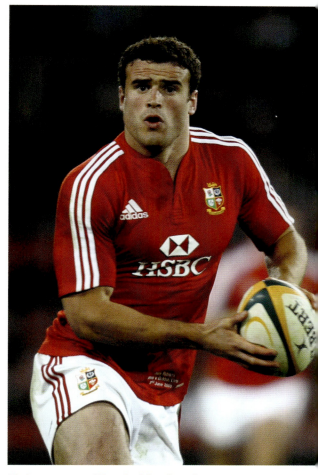

Roberts was still only 22 when he was chosen for his first Lions tour to South Africa in 1997

to look after himself in a physical sense, on and off the field.

He settled into playing full back and began training with Cardiff's academy in the sixth form, but there was always plenty more to his life than rugby. In cricket, he was a budding fast bowler with more pace than direction, and he was highly capable academically, showing a thirst for learning that would

Roberts and Phil Vickery celebrate after the Lions won the third Test against South Africa in Johannesburg, a match Roberts had missed through injury

later lead him to qualify as a doctor from Cardiff University, going on to study a master's degree in medical science at Cambridge University.

After impressing at full back in his early outings for Cardiff's first team, he made his Wales debut, shortly after turning 21, in the 2008 Six Nations game at home to Scotland on the wing. While his first international appearance went reasonably well, he found himself dropped by Gatland for the next match and had to wait for the summer tour to South Africa for his next opportunity. He had played a minor part in a grand slam for Wales, but he was still very much on the fringes of the team.

In South Africa, he won his second cap in a heavy defeat to the Springboks in Bloemfontein, starting at full back, but in the days before the next match in Pretoria he was pulled aside by Shaun Edwards, the defence coach. Edwards is a gruff Wiganer, who does not waste words, and Roberts was still getting to know him. He asked Roberts if he had ever played inside centre, to which the response was that he had played there once, for Cardiff Schools, when he was 15. 'I've spoken with Gats and Rob, and we're thinking of playing you at No12 at the weekend,' Edwards said. 'Happy with that?' Roberts was shocked, having just made his first Test start in his preferred position, and summoned a mumbled response: 'Yeah, why not.' At which point Edwards left the room. The matter had been settled by a decidedly one-way conversation. 'With that short exchange,' Roberts said, 'the course of my life changed completely.'

It took a few games, inevitably, before Roberts felt anywhere near comfortable in his new position, but he switched to playing No12 in club rugby with Cardiff and gradually grew accustomed to the requirements of the role. The first time he felt that this was a job in which he could potentially excel was after the most daunting of challenges, his first meeting with New Zealand at the Millennium Stadium. Still awaiting a first ever victory over the All Blacks, Wales were leading 9–6 at half-time and, although they went on to lose 29–9, Roberts made a couple of breaks against a world-class midfield that showed the progress he was making at No12.

Coming from a slightly wider position to pick a line between Ma'a Nonu, his opposite number, and Dan Carter, the fly half, Roberts punched holes in the All Blacks' defence. And if he could put Wales on the front foot against opponents of such quality, holding his own in defence as well, he was clearly making a fist of the No12 role. He was approached after the game by Edwards. 'Lad, you became a Test player today,' the defence coach said. Which, in the Wales camp at the time, was something near the height of praise.

The 2009 trip to South Africa was seen as a crucial one for the Lions. Their previous visit to New Zealand, four years earlier, had been an unqualified disaster, with a 3–0 defeat in the Test series and a heavy-handed attempt to over-professionalise the whole operation from Clive Woodward, the World Cup-winning England coach, that had spectacularly backfired. He had picked way too many players, separating the group crudely into Test players and the midweek team, and morale throughout the tour suffered badly as a result. Maintaining relations between those playing the biggest games and those left out has always been a barometer of success or failure for a Lions tour. There was little chemistry among the 2005 squad and a badly one-sided Test series was felt by some to jeopardise the whole Lions concept, with the modern calendar threatening to squeeze out such extended tours.

To address such concerns, McGeechan was brought back in as head coach in 2009, with Gatland as his forwards coach and Edwards marshalling the defence. Although he only had 12 caps to his name at the time, Roberts was chosen as one of the centres, as the Welsh supplied 12 of the 36-man party. With Tom Shanklin, his fellow Wales centre, ruled out by injury before the tour, Roberts felt that he had a chance of making the Test team if he could impress in the early tour fixtures.

The first time he played alongside Brian O'Driscoll was in the second game of the trip, against Golden Lions at Ellis Park. Within 10 minutes, it was becoming abundantly clear that something special was brewing between the touring team's two centres. The spark was lit as early as the sixth minute, O'Driscoll taking a pass from Stephen Jones, the fly half, 20 metres from the line. He jinked inside one defender and when he was wrapped up by a couple more despairing tackles, he looked up for support and found Roberts arriving at just the right moment, taking his partner's offload to dive over and score.

Four minutes later, as the red-shirted Lions attacked again, Roberts ran a decoy line that sucked in defenders, enabling Jones to find Tommy Bowe, who put O'Driscoll over by the posts. Here were the seeds of the blossoming relationship: even when they were not working directly together, Roberts was providing a threat that created the extra space in which O'Driscoll could be so dangerous. The Lions' coaches liked what they saw and Roberts immediately felt at home with his experienced ally. 'In our first game together, we dovetailed naturally, I was the yin to his yang,' he said. 'The direct, powerful ball carrier to his dextrous, pacy hot-stepper.'

Those qualities were then perfectly illustrated by the Lions' opening try in the first Test against South Africa in Durban, where the stands were awash with red shirts, simply mocking the idea that the Lions concept might be outdated. The travelling support for the Lions

After missing the first two Tests of the 2013 series in Australia through injury, Roberts was irresistible when he returned for the decisive third Test in Sydney

Roberts with the Tom Richards Cup after the Lions thrashed the Wallabies in the series decider in Sydney in 2013

forged on into the 22, stepped inside and handed on to Tom Croft to score. The two centres had combined in thrilling fashion to bring the Lions into the match and the series.

It was not just in attack that they combined, but in defence, too, as they mounted a tandem tackle on JP Pietersen, the Springboks' wing, that saw him driven back almost 20 yards. On this occasion, though, their efforts would not be enough. South Africa opened up a 26–7 lead, but the Lions hit back with late tries from Croft and Mike Phillips that reduced the final margin to five points and gave them great hope for the second Test.

Back at Loftus Versfeld in Pretoria, where Roberts had been converted into a centre a year earlier, the Lions maintained the momentum they had generated in the closing stages in Durban. O'Driscoll helped to set the tone with a huge hit on Victor Matfield, the mighty lock, and then the Lions scored a superb early try from Rob Kearney, the full back. They led 16–8 at half-time, which they extended to 19–8 after the break, before the Springboks began a comeback of their own. This took the form, initially, of a try from Bryan Habana, but in

was astonishing. After the home side had opened up an early lead, Roberts ran a straight line onto a pass from Jones 35 metres out, picking one of those angles between two defenders, leaving one trailing and the other clinging onto him. As he was stopped, he barely had to look up to find O'Driscoll, almost telepathically, right on his shoulder. O'Driscoll

a brutally physical game, the Lions began to lose men. Roberts and O'Driscoll had been exceptional once again, but both had to leave the field, O'Driscoll with concussion and Roberts with a wrist injury. The Lions also lost both their props, Adam Jones and Gethin Jenkins. When Roberts went to hospital after the game, he was one of five Lions requiring medical treatment.

The loss of so many key players turned the tide against the Lions. Ronan O'Gara had come on for Roberts and, with the scores locked on 25–25, he made a clumsy challenge on Fourie du Preez and Morné Steyn kicked a nerveless penalty to win the game for South Africa. Despite giving so much to an incredibly intense Test match, the Lions had lost the series. 'That was the worst I ever felt in the changing rooms after a match,' Roberts said. 'To lose a game of that magnitude after performing so well was soul-destroying.'

They had lost the series, but they would win the third Test and, more importantly, the Lions had enjoyed a compellingly successful tour overall, with a palpable spirit of togetherness among the squad and a wonderful bond with their fans. There was life in the Lions just yet.

Back with Wales, the team that Gatland had been building were growing in stature. At the World Cup in 2011, there was the narrow miss of an agonising 9–8 semi-final defeat to France after Sam Warburton had been sent off, but the second grand slam of Gatland's tenure came in 2012. During this time, Roberts had become the defensive captain for Wales, the player nominated by Edwards as his on-field lieutenant driving the team's defence system. But he was also seeking to improve his athleticism to ensure that his attacking game was as strong as his defence, that he would always be seen as more than just a muscular straight-line running machine.

With Wales' strength and conditioning coach, Adam Beard, Roberts worked to improve his running technique, so that he was more efficient, streamlined and altogether quicker into his stride. Such changes do not come about quickly or easily, they require long hours of monitoring and repetition, but Roberts had never been afraid of hard work. Against Italy in the Six Nations, he got a chance to show that those tweaks were taking effect. Taking a pass from Rhys Priestland 10 metres inside his own half, he accelerated through

Roberts scoring the Lions' fourth try in the third Test in Sydney, setting the seal on their series-clinching victory

a gap and sprinted 60 metres to score. He was never going to be a prolific try-scorer for Wales, so this was one, from distance, that he particularly enjoyed, feeling that the time devoted to honing his running technique was paying dividends.

The Six Nations in 2013 finished with another title for Wales, this time coming with the added bonus of playing England on the final day in Cardiff. England were chasing the grand slam at the time; Wales could not only stop them but overhaul them at the top of the table as well. A narrow defeat to Ireland in the opening round of matches had

prevented Wales chasing another grand slam, but since then they had tightened their defence, in particular. As his defensive captain, Edwards had wanted Roberts to lead that process after a defeat to Ireland in which they conceded 30 points.

Three wins later, the Millennium Stadium was at its most raucous for England's visit. Roberts made Wales' intentions clear with an early head-to-head tackle that stopped Manu Tuilagi, England's midfield bulldozer, dead in his tracks. Streaking away in the second half, Wales put in a rip-roaring performance, scoring two tries to none for a 30–3 victory that sealed the title. And the number of tries conceded by Wales in those last four games? Zero. To his great surprise, the defensive captain even earned a bottle of champagne from Edwards for his efforts.

Successive Six Nations titles ensured that Wales would have the largest contingent of players in the British & Irish Lions squad to tour Australia that summer, numbering 15 in a 37-man squad. With Wales, he had struck up a highly effective centre pairing with Jonathan Davies, not a classic light-footed No13, but a robust player, equally capable in attack and defence, who could play in either centre position. Davies was on the Lions tour, too, and when Roberts was ruled out of the first two Tests with a hamstring injury, Davies stepped into his shoes. He wore No12 and partnered Brian O'Driscoll, Roberts' old mate from 2009, who was making his fourth Lions tour, at the age of 34, in the hope of experiencing his first series win.

By the time of the third Test in Sydney, the series was level at 1–1 and Roberts was back in contention. When Gatland asked him if he would be ready to start, he was not absolutely sure of the condition of his hamstring and the doubts continued to plague him until the morning of the match. But he decided, on balance, that he would be fit. Aside from the small matter of a Lions series decider, there was extra pressure on the centre pairing, because O'Driscoll had made way for Roberts' return, with Davies switching to No13. Irish fans were in uproar, but Gatland felt his Welsh centres were a more effective defensive pairing. The magic of 2009 between Roberts and O'Driscoll would not be rekindled.

Both Davies and Roberts were outstanding on that night in Sydney, Roberts racing across the line for a triumphant try in the second half, picking a lovely line onto Conor Murray's pass, handing off Will Genia and racing away, as the Lions romped home 41–16, ending that long wait for a series win. 'It was an amazing feeling in that changing room, just utter ecstasy,' Roberts said. 'Champagne bottles were popping, James Bond [the actor Daniel Craig] was there, the family were in the stands. That's why you play the game, for those moments.'

J Williams, *who carried his athleticism from the track to the rugby field.*

JJ WILLIAMS

Name	JJ Williams
Birthdate	1 April 1948 (died 29 October 2020)
Birthplace	Maesteg
Country	Wales (30 caps)
Position	Left wing – No11
Lions caps	7

Remarkably quick, Williams was seen at his best in the Lions' epic series win in South Africa in 1974, when his eye for the tryline saw him score four memorable tries.

It does not take an expert on rugby to recognise the prime asset that JJ Williams brought to a team. There have been plenty of sprinters whose raw pace has seemed to lend itself to playing on the wing, without having the game understanding to make the most of their speed. But Williams, although he was an accomplished athlete before he made his name as a winger, was a rugby player blessed with the speed of a sprinter. His reading of the game and the understanding he forged with his teammates were such that his speed of thought was almost as impressive as his turn of pace, which really was breathtaking, making him

such an important player in those dominant Wales teams of the 1970s, as well as for the British Lions on the tours to South Africa in 1974 and New Zealand three years later.

So often Williams' tries seemed to feature a bouncing ball. Sometimes he was the one who reacted the quickest when others were waiting around for the bounce, scooping up loose possession and using his speed to disappear off into the distance. But he was also an absolute master at the chip and chase, finding pockets of space behind defenders and forcing them to turn, then racing past them to gather. It is a tricky skill to perform with any degree of precision while

Williams scores for Llanelli against Cardiff. He moved from Bridgend to play for the Scarlets so that he could benefit from the wisdom of Carwyn James, the former Lions coach

on the move; all the more so when you are moving at Williams' pace.

This was how he scored the try in Port Elizabeth that confirmed the Lions' momentous series victory over the Springboks in 1974. That was his second try of the game, following two that he had scored in the previous win in Pretoria. Much of the talk after that historic tour was about the performances of the Lions' forwards and the brutally physical nature of the contests, but rarely has a winger had such an impact on a series.

The tour to South Africa actually came relatively early in his international career. He had won only six caps for Wales at that stage, having made his debut, aged 24, against France in Paris the year before, then established himself in the side during the 1974 Five Nations championship, scoring tries against Ireland and France, forming the potent back three with Gerald Davies and JPR Williams that would become so familiar, and earning himself selection for the Lions in the process.

Four summers earlier, he had been competing on the international stage in a different sport, representing Wales at the Commonwealth Games in Edinburgh. Athletics had been a twin passion with rugby in his younger years, growing up in Maesteg with his father, Albert, a bus driver, his mother, Elizabeth, and his older brother, Peter. He attended the local grammar school before moving on to Cardiff College of Education, a sporting hotbed that had also produced Gareth Edwards, the Wales scrum half, and Lynn Davies, gold medal winner in the long jump at the 1964 Tokyo Olympics.

It was with his running spikes on that Williams first sprung to prominence. He had won the British Schools titles at 100 metres and 200 metres, and at the Commonwealth Games, aged 22, he competed in those two events along with the 4 x 100 metre relay. In the 100 metres, he clocked a time of 10.67 seconds, finishing fifth in his heat and narrowly missing out on qualifying for the quarter-finals. He went one better in the 200 metres, finishing third in his heat in 21.4 seconds before coming seventh in the quarter-final. In the relay, the Welsh quartet, which included Lynn Davies on the second leg and Williams on the third, reached the final and finished fifth, only 0.2 second away from a medal.

Later in life, his three children would all follow him into athletics. While James was a middle-distance runner, both Kathryn and Rhys specialised in 400 metres hurdles, Kathryn becoming a British junior international and Rhys going further still, winning silver at the European Championships in Barcelona in 2010 and then going one step higher on the podium two years later in Helsinki, where he became European champion.

Despite his athletic prowess, though, Williams Snr always felt his heart was with rugby and, after the Commonwealth Games in Edinburgh, set his mind to playing for Wales. 'I realised when I got to 21 that I could be a good British standard athlete, but I would never be a world star,' he said. 'So I went back to rugby and it was obviously a good move. Rugby was in my blood.' Having initially left Maesteg for Bridgend, for whom he scored 99 tries in 100 matches, to further his international ambitions he moved in 1972 to play for Llanelli under Carwyn James, the great coach who had masterminded the

It was a try from nothing, an indication of his ability to create magical moments.

Lions' first ever series victory in New Zealand the previous year.

The move proved to be smart. In the first few weeks of his time with Llanelli at Stradey Park, he played in the legendary 9–3 victory over the touring All Blacks, an unforgettable day for a proud rugby town, a game still talked about by those who were there. The whole town seemed to be in the ground, thousands more claimed to have been, and the game was immortalised by Max Boyce in his poem, simply entitled *9–3*:

'Those that went to Stradey, boys,
Will remember 'til they die
How New Zealand were defeated
And how the pubs ran dry.'

After the game, the crowd swarmed onto the pitch, mobbing their heroes and it took the players an age to make it to the dressing room. Even there the locals were keen to celebrate with the players who had just become local legends. 'I think half of Llanelli was in that dressing room, it was crazy, wonderful,' Williams said. 'Carwyn brought 15 club boys together to beat the might of the All Blacks.'

He was just John Williams at this point, his initials coming into their own once he made it into the Wales team alongside the other John Williams and, to spare confusion, they were henceforth JPR and JJ to the entire rugby world. It was only months after that victory over the All Blacks that they were picked in the same Wales team, as JJ made his debut as a replacement against France in Paris. He won his second cap against Australia in November 1973 and then nailed down his place during the Five Nations later that season, given the chance to familiarise himself with JPR at full back and Gerald Davies on the other wing, and to show what he could do.

By the standards of the 1970s, it was not a vintage Five Nations for Wales, as they began by beating Scotland, then drew with both Ireland and France before losing to England at Twickenham. Wales scored only four tries in their four matches, but Williams scored two of them and began to serve notice of his ability on the international stage.

His first try for his country, against Ireland in Dublin, was a neat score with a straightforward finish, Gareth Edwards breaking to the blindside of a scrum and sending Williams clear from 15 metres out. His second international try, against France in Cardiff two weeks later, was more of a sign of things to come.

There seemed to be little danger to France as Wales moved the ball to the left wing, where Williams took a pass 40 metres out with two French defenders in front of him. But he spotted a sliver of space outside his opposite number, Roland Bertranne, and threaded a deft little grubber kick past him with the outside of his right boot. As he skirted around Bertranne, the ball sat up and Williams managed to knee the ball over Jean-Michel Aguirre, the covering full back, sprinting past him to gather and score. It was a try from nothing, an indication of his ability to create magical moments, and early evidence of that kick and chase that would become such a trademark. He later judged it the best try of the 12 he scored in 30 appearances for Wales and it put him on the path towards a Lions tour.

There was another Williams kick and chase in Wales' final game of the 1974 Five Nations, when they needed a win at Twickenham to take the title, but this one did not end quite so happily. As a Wales attack threatened to founder near the halfway line, Williams picked up the loose ball and spotted a gap in the England defence. He accelerated through and chipped over Dusty Hare, the England full back. The kick was well weighted, coming to rest just over the line, and he was a fraction ahead of the two covering English wingers, David Duckham and Peter Squires. He dived to touch down, with the two Englishmen diving either side of him, and was sure he had scored. But the Irish referee, John West, had other ideas, and awarded a 22-metre drop-out to England, denying Williams another try from nothing. The winger, his teammates and the Welsh contingent in the Twickenham crowd could not quite believe the decision. 'I was livid,' he said.

Wales lost the game 16–12, but Williams had announced himself to a wider audience and he was duly selected for the Lions tour to South Africa, where the touring team had not won a series since 1896. The Lions were unbeaten in seven provincial matches leading up to the first Test, including a thumping 97–0 victory over South West Districts in Mossel Bay, in which Williams scored six tries, equalling the Lions record set by David Duckham in New Zealand three years earlier.

The first Test, in Cape Town, was played on a bog of a pitch, with the Lions prevailing 12–3 in a hard-fought, tryless contest. But the rest of the series was played on bone-hard pitches that rewarded running rugby and favoured a team that happened to have a lightning-quick winger in their line-up. The second Test was on the high veld in Pretoria, played on a straw-coloured pitch, and it was from a scrum just inside South Africa's half that the Lions scored their first try. Picking up from the base of the scrum, Edwards kicked over his shoulder down the left wing. Williams was expecting it and set off in pursuit, haring past Chris Pope, the Springbok right wing, as though his opposite number was merely jogging. Ian McCallum, the full back, did not quite arrive in time and Williams toed the bouncing ball past him before gathering to score. That kick and chase again, even if the initial boot this time came from Edwards. He was thriving on those hard grounds.

Before half-time, Williams added a second try, crowning a thrilling counterattack from deep started by Phil Bennett, the Llanelli and Wales fly half. In his inimitable way, Bennett slalomed his way out of his own 22 and the momentum was continued by Willie John McBride, Mervyn Davies and Edwards. The movement seemed to have foundered when the ball went to ground, and some of the Springboks slowed as the ball trickled towards the right-hand touchline.

But Williams suddenly appeared from the opposite wing. He was alive to the fact that the referee had not blown his whistle, so he hacked ahead, not once but twice, away from the despairing arms of Gerald Bosch, and was able to pick up and score again. Once more, his speed of thought and fleetness of foot had combined to great effect, once more he had been the quickest to react to the loose ball, this time on the other side of the field to where he was stationed. 'JJ Williams, where's he come from?' was the astonished cry from Nigel Starmer-Smith, the television commentator.

A record 28–9 victory put the Lions 2–0 up, meaning that a third victory in Port Elizabeth would clinch the four-match series. That third Test would turn out to be one of the most violent in history as the Springboks set out to intimidate the Lions with the ferocity of their pack, and the match was scarred by a mass brawl in each half.

Williams squeezes into the left corner to score Wales' only try against France in Cardiff in 1976, the crucial victory on the way to their grand slam

Somehow, though, on another firm pitch, the Lions managed to keep their composure sufficiently to play some scintillating rugby.

After a try from Gordon Brown had given the Lions a 7–3 half-time lead, the Lions launched a move from a lineout on the right, which was palmed down by Brown to Edwards. The ball was then moved smoothly left, through Bennett, Ian McGeechan and Dick Milliken, whose long pass sent Williams on his way. Just before he was tackled, he passed inside to JPR Williams, then tracked back inside and took a return inside pass from JPR. There was still work to be done, but he stepped inside the last couple

of defenders to complete a quite brilliant try. The speed at which the move was carried out utterly flummoxed the Springboks and Williams was relishing the hard ground. 'JJ loved it because it was like being back on the athletics track,' said Bennett. 'He knew no one would catch him and they couldn't even get close.'

The Lions were almost there and Williams' next try removed any doubt. Receiving the ball just inside his own half on the left wing, he immediately looked up, saw space behind the Springboks' defence and kicked ahead. The kick was beautifully weighted, he left three turning defenders

*Williams takes the field before Wales'
Five Nations match against England at
Cardiff in 1977*

trailing in his wake, and got a kind bounce 10 metres from the line, gratefully scooping the ball up and diving over to touch down. No other player before in the 20th century had scored two tries in a Lions Test, now Williams had just done it in consecutive games and the series was won. The final Test in Johannesburg was a draw and the Lions had gone through the entire tour unbeaten, one of the greatest achievements in the history of British and Irish rugby.

Back home, Williams continued to play his part in the Wales team that dominated the Five Nations in the 1970s, winning titles in 1975 and 1976, the second of which came with a memorable grand slam, and Williams further distinguished himself with a hat-trick of tries in a 28–3 drubbing of Australia. He had given up his job as a teacher after his employers would not grant him leave of absence for the 1974 Lions tour, moving into marketing instead. His second Lions tour, to New Zealand in 1977, was not as successful collectively as the first – how could it have been? – but Williams still played his part in helping the Lions stay in the series until the end.

> Williams was not just quick, he moved with grace, gliding past defenders in pursuit of those clever chips ahead.

The series was a low-scoring, forward-dominated affair, with the Lions scoring only three tries in four Tests. After losing the first match in Wellington 16–12, the touring team bounced back with a win full of character in Christchurch. Williams scored the only try of the game, having been switched to the right wing, and it showcased the breadth of his skillset, sometimes overlooked because his pace was so startling.

Before half-time, the Lions were attacking down the right, but running out of room, with Williams taking a pass from McGeechan with only Andy Irvine outside him and three All Blacks defenders blocking their path. But Williams dummied to pass to Irvine, stepping off his right foot in the same instant and sending all three All Blacks the wrong way. He sprinted through the gap he had created and the Lions had a lead they would not relinquish. The series was to end in disappointment, as the Lions lost the last two matches and Williams injured his hamstring during the third Test, ruling him out of the fourth, but his tally of five tries in seven Tests had secured his place in Lions history.

He would retire at the age of 30 to build the industrial painting company that became extremely successful, but he finished his international career in particularly fitting fashion. The Five Nations in 1979 concluded with a title decider between England and Wales in Cardiff, but England never came close. Wales won 27–3 and Williams set the seal on the victory, taking a pass from David Richards 20 metres from the line, with space to run into, and no English defender was able to lay a hand on him.

Williams was not just quick, he moved with grace, gliding past defenders in pursuit of those clever chips ahead. But he was also blessed with the sharpest of rugby brains, spotting space and try-scoring opportunities before others had cottoned on. It was a telling combination that made for one of the greatest wings the game has seen.

Barry John, pictured before the 1971 Lions series in New Zealand that would change his life

BARRY JOHN

Name	Barry John
Birthdate	6 January 1945 (died 4 February 2024)
Birthplace	Cefneithin
Country	Wales (25 caps)
Position	Fly half – No10
Lions caps	5

A masterful tactician and game manager at fly half, he could exploit opposing teams' weaknesses with his boot and torment them with his running game.

It is often said that Barry John was rugby's first superstar. Stepping off the plane from their groundbreaking tour of New Zealand in 1971, the All Blacks vanquished for the first time, the British & Irish Lions players discovered that the widespread radio and growing television coverage of their exciting exploits on the other side of the world had created a level of fame and recognition previously unknown to rugby players, all of whom were amateurs with a full-time job to return to during the week.

The rugby that John, in particular, played on that tour had not only been resolutely effective, but also carried immense aesthetic appeal. Rugby union is a game that, when it is played badly, in wet and muddy conditions, provides a spectacle that only a mother could love. When it is played well, powerful forwards combining seamlessly with swift and skilful backs, it can be a thing of real beauty. As the fly half sparking the Lions' brilliant backline into life in New Zealand, in addition to his own elusive running and pinpoint kicking, John played a starring role not only in beating the All Blacks in their own backyard, which remains the outstanding achievement in Lions' history, but also spreading the gospel of rugby itself.

John played a starring role not only in beating the All Blacks in their own backyard . . . but also spreading the gospel of rugby itself.

He returned from that tour having been anointed King John by a New Zealand audience who were notoriously hard to please. 'His tactical appreciation and general game in New Zealand were astonishing,' John Dawes, the tour captain, said. 'He really came of age on that tour and developed an incredible self-confidence. He just took New Zealand by the scruff of the neck.'

After being forced home with injury early in the previous Lions tour, to South Africa in 1968, John had already gone some way towards kick-starting a Welsh era of dominance in the Five Nations championship. Forging one of the game's great half-back partnerships with Gareth Edwards, both for club and country, he helped Wales to win Five Nations titles in 1969 and 1971. That was a team full of players who would become household names in Wales, where the game is a national obsession, both for

their triumphs with the national team and then on tour with the Lions. But John would not share in the later success of that era, with grand slams in 1976 and 1978, nor would he go on tour with the Lions again to South Africa in 1974, as so many of his Welsh teammates did.

At the age of 27, tiring of the growing intrusion that fame had brought, he hung up his boots, never to play again. He had won only 25 caps for Wales, a staggeringly meagre haul for such a great player. But the amount that he had achieved over those 25 matches, and over his five Test appearances for the Lions, comfortably exceeded what many players accomplish in twice as many games. 'If you loved rugby,' JPR Williams said, 'then you loved watching BJ.'

One of the curiosities of that 1971 tour to New Zealand was that the Lions' playmaker, Barry John, and the coach, Carwyn James, hailed from the same tiny place, the village of Cefneithin, a few miles north of Llanelli. John had been unsure about travelling to New Zealand after a physical Five Nations, but James' presence helped to persuade him. Their philosophies, as well as their background, were perfectly aligned for that tour, with James determined that a gifted set of backs would take the game to the All Blacks, while John's attacking flair was the ideal conduit for such a game.

There are not many places in the world where a small secondary school could boast two former international players among their staff, but that was the case for John when he went to Gwendraeth Grammar, where the head, William John Jones, had won one cap as a flanker, and the PE teacher, Ray Williams, had won three caps on the wing. Williams, in particular, who scored more than 200 tries for Llanelli, helped to nurture John's early love for the game.

The son of a coal miner, like so many of his peers, John grew up with three brothers and two sisters. He was the second to arrive, three years after his older brother, and both his younger brothers, Alan and Clive, would go on to play for Llanelli. They all played for the village team and their school and Barry's talent soon saw him gravitate to playing for Llanelli, where he made his first-team debut aged 18, and quickly developed a reputation for striking match-winning drop-goals. One of those came against the touring Australia team, to which

John in preparation with Wales for the match against South Africa in Cardiff in 1970, which they drew 6–6

he added a try as Llanelli recorded a famous victory over the Wallabies.

After leaving school, John trained as a teacher at Trinity College in Carmarthen, and then took a job as a teacher in Cardiff, prompting him to leave Llanelli. Moving to Cardiff, he found himself sharing a house with Gerald Davies, and would

John sets off on one of those elusive runs during Wales' victory over England at Twickenham in 1970

strike up that deadly half-back combination with Gareth Edwards.

The story goes that before they were first to play together, Edwards insisted on some extra practice, to help him get to know his new partner's game. The communication and timing of movements between a scrum half and fly half can make a whole team come together. 'You chuck it, I'll catch it,' was John's response, which told Edwards something about the man who would play outside him so many times. 'When I heard those words, I knew this was the guy

I wanted to play with,' Edwards said. 'There was a confidence about that statement, I knew that no matter how I threw it to him, he would catch it. We only improved as we got to know each other better.'

Aged 21, John made his international debut against Australia in Cardiff in December 1966, but was then dropped after his second game, against Scotland, as the selectors reverted to David Watkins, a more experienced fly half. Watkins though would defect to rugby league, and John was given the chance to nail down his position as the regular No10 in the 1968 Five Nations. In the opening game away to England at Twickenham, the new half-back pairing began to show what they were capable of, with Edwards scoring a try and, as Wales battled their way back from 11–3 down, John struck one of those trademark drop-goals, late in the game, to earn his side a draw.

Both John and Edwards did enough in four Five Nations appearances that year to be chosen for the Lions' squad to tour South Africa in the summer, although neither would last long. After an encouraging start to the trip, the Cardiff and Wales half backs were chosen to start together for the first Test in Pretoria. Midway through the first half, John was upended in a tackle by Jan Ellis, the fearsome Springbok flanker, and broke his collarbone as he landed on the hard ground, ending his tour. The Lions lost that match and then drew the second Test in Port Elizabeth, after which Edwards succumbed to injury as well.

By now, the ingredients of that special Wales team were coming together. Gerald Davies and John Taylor had also toured with the Lions, and Mervyn Davies and JPR Williams were about to arrive on the scene in the 1969 Five Nations. John's confidence in his ability on the international stage was growing and that showed in Wales' opening 17–3 defeat of Scotland at Murrayfield. Wales had already scored two tries and Colin Telfer, the Scotland fly half, was attempting to clear his lines when his kick was charged down by John, who then nonchalantly scooped the ball up. There was only Colin Blaikie, the Scotland full back, between him and the tryline and he had Gerald Davies free to his right. John shaped to pass to Davies but threw an outrageous dummy instead that left Blaikie floundering and gave him a free run to the line. The showman in John was beginning to unveil some of his tricks.

A victory over Ireland and a draw with France meant a title showdown in their final match with England in Cardiff. After giving the pass for the first of a remarkable haul of four tries for Maurice Richards, John himself began to weave some magic. Picking up a bouncing ball 25 metres out, John stepped inside Ken Plummer, the England wing, then stepped off his left foot to sway inside first one and then another defender to score. There was an effortlessness in the way that, holding the ball in two hands, he was able to ghost past the attempted tackles, with barely a hand laid on him, an evasiveness that was to become a real hallmark of his game.

Wales ran out comprehensive 30–9 winners that day, clinching the first of two Five Nations titles in three years. In 1971, that great team was approaching its full potential, beginning with a 22–6 victory over England that featured two John drop-goals. There was the close shave against Scotland at Murrayfield, with John scoring the third of his side's four tries, hacking a loose ball down the left touchline, then picking up and leaving several Scots trailing in his wake. So often it seemed as though he was within defenders' grasp, so often they were unable to pin him down.

The chance to clinch the grand slam came against France in Paris. A low-scoring game was in the balance when Wales won a scrum against the head in front of the French posts, from which Edwards broke left and fed John. At first, it seemed as though there could be no way through, with three France players in front of him, but he accelerated outside Jean-Louis Berot, his opposite number, and inside Jean-Pierre Lux to coast

over the line, sealing a 9–5 win and a first Welsh grand slam for 19 years. The task of containing John was proving beyond most opponents.

Inevitably, given this burgeoning reputation, he would be a marked man on tour to New Zealand with the Lions. Before the Test series, hungry provincial players would be primed to do the All Blacks a favour by knocking the Lions' playmaker down a notch or two. But that was if they could get their hands on him. In one tour match, on a muddy pitch against New Zealand Universities, he received the ball 25 metres out, shaped to drop a goal off his right foot, but instead set off to his left, bemusing four advancing defenders. He then stepped off his left foot, leaving another would-be tackler on his backside, then jinking inside again to leave another opponent in the mud. To a man, the floored defenders turned round to see John touching down between the posts. There was that elusiveness again, a fluidity of movement that moved one journalist to write in *The Scotsman*, having encountered John after a match: 'What a relief it was to see Barry John leaving by the door, rather than simply drifting through the wall.'

As coach, Carwyn James knew of John's importance to the shape of his Test team. He was left out of the tour match against Canterbury, which James had correctly anticipated to be a violent affair, and on the odd occasion when John was not relishing a fitness session, he was cut a little slack. 'One time we went on a cross-country run through a wood,' Ian McLauchlan, the Lions prop, said. 'When we came out the other side to a long stretch of road back to where we started, we saw a flatbed lorry driving by with Barry sitting in the back. If anyone else did that, Carwyn would have lost the plot, but Barry got away with it. "I play with my brain," he'd say. And that was the way it was.'

Come the first Test, the Lions had still not been beaten in New Zealand, and the All Blacks tore out of the blocks in Dunedin, only for the Lions to score first, much against the run of play, through McLauchlan's charge down. The Lions were tackling their hearts out, the home side dominated possession, but whenever they surrendered the ball they found that John kicked them to distraction, giving his side a territorial foothold that continued to frustrate the All

Long after his retirement, which came so suddenly at the age of 27, Barry John's autograph was much sought after in Wales

Blacks. He kicked to the corners, turning New Zealand's wings and giving Fergie McCormick, the full back, a torrid afternoon.

Two years earlier, Wales had been on tour to New Zealand, and had been badly beaten twice by the All Blacks. In the second of those games, a thumping 33–12 defeat for Wales in Auckland, McCormick kicked a world record 24 points. It was a sobering trip all round for the Welsh.

Now John was taking a measure of revenge on McCormick, turning

The Lions return victorious from their series victory over the All Blacks in 1971. Barry John is extreme right, with Doug Smith, the manager, in the centre and John Dawes, the captain, to his right

him this way and that, and the All Blacks' struggles to deal with the precision of this kicking game saw them concede two penalty goals to John, which, in addition to McLauchlan's try, saw the Lions to a 9–3 victory. 'It was as if he was guiding the ball by remote control,' McCormick said later, ruefully. He was dropped for the second Test and never played for New Zealand again.

The All Blacks bounced back to win the second Test, although the Lions' attacking game was in decent order, with Gerald Davies' two fine tries, and so they went to the third Test in Wellington with plenty of belief. This was a game they were desperate to win, and this time the Lions made the quicker

start and within 13 minutes, they had established a substantial lead. In the third minute, John put his side on the scoreboard with a sweetly struck drop-goal from right on the 22. Six minutes later, Edwards broke to the blindside to put Davies into the corner, and then John scored himself, as Edwards took lineout ball on the right, handed off Bob Burgess and found his half-back partner right on his shoulder to run in for the try.

With a thirteen-point cushion, John was able to call on his tactical kicking game once again to make the All Blacks chase the game from distance. They managed a solitary try from Laurie Mains, but that was all, and a 13–3 victory meant the Lions could not lose the series. 'King John wins game for the Lions,' ran the headlines in the New Zealand papers. The nickname stuck and the Lions players began to bow in his presence, although it was not a moniker with which he was ever entirely comfortable. The fourth Test was a hard-fought affair and a 14–14 draw gave the Lions the ultimate prize of a series win in New Zealand.

After his performances in winning a grand slam, John had come into the series with belief high in his own game, and from the pivotal position that spread out across the rest of the team. They were a talented bunch and John brought the best out of them, as well as himself. 'Playing with Barry gave you so much confidence, he was the conductor of our orchestra and such a calming influence,' JPR Williams said. 'I believe that Barry was the best ever in his position.' Edwards, meanwhile, felt the surging belief from his partner. 'Physically he was perfectly made for the job, strong from the hips down and firm but slender from the waist to the shoulders,' Edwards said. 'One success on the field bred another and soon he gave off a cool superiority which spread to others in the side.'

Little did those teammates know at the time that John would be calling time on his career before long. The adulation that came with that 1971 triumph was lapped up at first, but the constant attention became a gnawing annoyance to John. He was also being offered jobs that would compromise his amateur status, including a role writing for the *Daily Express.* He played three matches in the 1972 Five Nations, all of which were won, but they did not play a fourth, as the Troubles were escalating in Northern Ireland, and the tournament remained incomplete.

With that, at the age of 27, John retired, leaving rugby fans everywhere to marvel at what he had achieved and the way he had played the game, but also to wonder about how much more there might have been to come from a talent that had shimmered so brightly and brought the sport as a whole to a wider audience. 'He was just about reaching his zenith then,' Mervyn Davies said. 'He should have stayed in rugby a damn sight longer.'

Gareth Edwards, an unquestionably great scrum half, who might have excelled in any number of positions

GARETH EDWARDS

Name	Gareth Edwards
Birthdate	12 July 1947
Birthplace	Gwaun-Cae-Gurwen
Country	Wales (53 caps)
Position	Scrum half – No9
Lions caps	10

With the acceleration of a winger and the strength of a forward, Edwards could probably have played in any position he chose. That he also possessed fine handling and kicking skills made him a true one-off as a scrum half.

One sure measure of the impact that Gareth Edwards made during his international career, spanning just over a decade with Wales and the British & Irish Lions, is that any discussion of his historical standing is not limited simply to where he ranks among the game's finest scrum halves. It tends to be taken as read that he sits at the top of any ranking of the best No9s the game has seen. The recent emergence of Antoine Dupont, the gifted totem of a resurgent French team, has added a new layer to the debate, but Edwards has long been widely considered to be the best player we have ever seen in his position, one who would be as effective in any other era as he was in his own.

The broader discussion is whether Edwards was the greatest player the game has ever seen. The variety of positional requirements and differences in the game from one generation to another mean that such a question can never be satisfactorily answered, but when it is asked, or when lists of contenders are compiled, Edwards' name features frequently.

To many people, he was the emblem of the Welsh golden era of the 1970s, with an ability to turn a game in any number of ways.

Gareth Edwards, in action here against Scotland in 1970, gave his fly half an extra split-second of time with the speed and precision of his service

On wet and muddy days, which are not unknown in the Upper Swansea Valley where he grew up, he had a varied kicking game that could shape a game, in both attack and defence, or with the occasional opportunistic drop-goal. His pass was long and precise and gave his fly half that crucial extra split-second. With ball in hand, his timing of a run and his acceleration could be startling, particularly when he was playing behind a dominant pack. And he was blessed with a strength rarely seen in scrum halves, punching way beyond his 5ft 10in and 13 stone, which enabled him to ward off the attention of so many voracious forwards who had pinned a target on his back. He was also, for good measure, the scorer of perhaps the most famous try in history.

His half-back partnerships with Barry John and Phil Bennett were the stuff of legend, both for Wales and the Lions, bringing the national team three grand slams during Edwards' time and the Lions series victories in New Zealand and South Africa. But both those magical fly halves, along with the rest of their teammates, knew they had been lucky to play with Edwards. 'His service to his fly half was near perfect and his speed of thought was matched by his speed over the ground,' JPR Williams, the Wales and Lions full back, said. 'His kicking was of the highest standard and he had such a low centre of gravity that he could get under any tackle. There simply was not a weakness to his game.'

Supporters of Swansea City might be forgiven for seeing such a talented athlete as one that got away. When he was 16, Edwards had the option of signing a contract to turn professional with his local professional football club, a dozen or so miles down the valley from his family home in Gwaun-Cae-Gurwen. He was a prolific goal scorer for his junior team, Colbren Rovers, and signing for the Swans would have brought an extra income to the family home from an early age. But his PE teacher at the local secondary school, Bill Samuel, although he was a former professional goalkeeper himself, believed that Edwards' footballing skills were exceeded by his ability with an oval ball and felt he could earn himself a scholarship at Millfield School, a prestigious English institution with a strong sporting reputation.

Samuel pushed hard for the scholarship and Edwards' family scraped together all they could to pay their part of the fees, even selling the family caravan, and he was eventually persuaded to move to Millfield for his sixth form years.

Until that point, he had been rooted in the community of his village, where his father, Glan, was a miner who loved rugby, but had been unable to play himself after losing his own father aged 13, forcing him to begin work at an early age. Edwards attended the local primary school and went on to Pontardawe Technical School, where he came under Samuels' wing, playing rugby for the school and the nearest club, Cwmgors. At Millfield, he not only honed his rugby skills, but excelled at gymnastics and athletics, winning the British Schools 220 yards hurdles title and becoming Welsh national long jump champion. Clearly, he was a gifted athlete, but rugby was where his affections lay. After Millfield, he moved to Cardiff College of Education to train to become a teacher, and joined Cardiff Rugby Club, which was where his serious rugby began.

In fact, such was the impression he had made playing for his college, that

Edwards had played only a handful of games for Cardiff before he was called up to make his international debut, still only 19, away against France in the 1967 Five Nations. He became a regular in the side the following year, darting over for a try that helped Wales to draw with England at Twickenham, and kicking a controversial drop-goal against Ireland in Dublin, which, to Irish eyes at least, had sailed wide of the posts.

The promise he had shown was reflected in his selection for the Lions' tour to South Africa and he performed well enough in the provincial matches to start the first two Tests. Although a hamstring injury intervened and prevented him from playing a further part in the series, which was lost 3–0 with one match drawn, it had given him precious experience both of the environment of a Lions tour, which he would draw on in New Zealand three years later, and of what was required to succeed in South Africa, which would come in handy in 1974.

With Wales, his half-back partnership with Barry John was blossoming and Edwards was performing with ever greater confidence. In the Five Nations in 1969, Wales went to play Paris in France with their title hopes intact

and Edwards was hugely influential in securing an 8–8 draw for his side and, in the manner that would become so familiar over the next decade, he demonstrated his knack for making a delayed run in support of a teammate, then accelerating to inject momentum to the move. As John Taylor was tackled on France's 22 on the right, Edwards popped up on his shoulder, surged down the wing, sidestepped inside one tackle, bounced off another, then took two more defenders over the line with him, a remarkable show of strength. Scrum halves are not supposed to be quite so difficult to bring down.

There was a similar display of strength, pace and tenacity in the try he scored against Scotland at Murrayfield in 1971, as Wales took another step towards the first of those three grand slams in eight years with a nail-biting win. When he picked up a flicked pass from Dai Morris at the base of a ruck 25 metres out, there seemed to be no danger, with a host of dark-blue shirts between him and the tryline. He set off first in an arcing run to the right, apparently heading for the corner flag, then stepped deftly inside at pace. The Scottish defence were wrong-footed, and when Edwards then stepped up

Edwards prepares a clearance kick against Ireland in the 1975 Five Nations, which brought the first of three titles in four seasons for Wales towards the end of his career

another gear again to accelerate to the line, they were left grasping at shadows. From next to nothing, he had conjured a try for Wales.

Over the course of the 1970s, some mighty tussles would play out between Wales and France, the two outstanding sides of the time, and the Welsh went to Paris in 1971 needing a victory to complete that grand slam. As was the case from time to time throughout his career, Edwards had been troubled by a sore hamstring, but was determined to play on. The decisive moment came when JPR Williams, 10 metres from his own line, smartly intercepted a pass from Roger Bourgarel and set off upfield. Haring down the left touchline, he made it into French territory, but looked to be running

out of steam, with two defenders covering across. He stepped inside, then suddenly heard a call outside him, where Edwards appeared, seemingly from nowhere, to take the pass and dive over in the corner.

The French hung their heads, a potentially match-winning attack of their own turned into a length-of-the-field try for their opponents. 'How Gareth got there, I will never know,' Williams said. 'He'd been suffering from hamstring problems, but Gareth being Gareth, he made sure that he was there when it mattered.'

He was still only 23 at the time, due to turn 24 during the Lions' tour of New Zealand that summer. In the Test matches, he would be coming up against Sid Going, the All Blacks scrum half, whom New Zealanders rated the best in the

Edwards gets his pass away for Wales against Ireland in the Five Nations in Cardiff in 1975

world at the time, and his elusive running had been a feature of Wales' two heavy defeats in New Zealand two years earlier. Edwards against Going was set to be one of the key battles of the series, but it would be influenced, as ever, by which pack gave their scrum half the better ball.

In the first Test, though, Edwards did not last long until those recurring niggles with his hamstring forced him off during the first half. The Lions won that first Test, but lost the second, with Going among the All Blacks' try-scorers, making the third Test a game of immense importance. As great players tend to do, Edwards raised his game when the stakes were high, producing one of the great Lions performances in a 13–3 win in Wellington.

Both of the Lions' tries were created by Edwards. The first came when, 10 yards from the All Blacks' line, the Lions rucked over scrappy lineout ball, and Edwards immediately sensed an opportunity to the blindside. Calling for quick ball from John Pullin, the hooker, Edwards broke to the right, where Gerald Davies was waiting, and a perfectly weighted pass from his scrum half put him outside his man and into the corner, with Going among the defenders arriving a fraction of a second too late. Shortly afterwards, Edwards showed his dynamism and strength at the tail of the lineout, where he could be so dangerous. Picking up a bouncing ball palmed down by John Taylor, he powerfully handed off Bob Burgess, burst past Baker Cottrell, and by the time Going got to his opposite number, the damage was done, as Edwards slipped a pass to Barry John on his shoulder and the Lions had scored again. That Test victory would prove to be decisive, with the final Test drawn and there was little doubt, now, to any objective observer, about who was the best scrum half in the world.

If Edwards was chiefly a creator in that vital third Test, back in Cardiff he would go on to show the full extent of his skill with some spectacular tries of his own. One particular score, against Scotland in the 1972 Five Nations, has a secure place in Welsh rugby folklore. On a wet, muddy day at the Arms Park, the move began when Mervyn Davies, his close ally at No8, laid back the ball on Wales' own 22-metre line, and Edwards swiftly spotted space around the right-hand side of the maul, handing off Rodger Arneil to set him on his way. He accelerated into the Scotland half and, realising he had no support, kicked over the head of the oncoming full back, Arthur Brown. Pursued by three more Scottish defenders, he kicked the loose ball ahead, winning the race to touch down by millimetres, completing a thrilling score in the mud-soaked corner. Edwards hurt himself in the act of scoring and was down for a short while, but when he was back on his feet, his whole face caked in mud, the stadium rose as one to applaud an incredible try.

And then, a year later, there was *that* try. You know the one. The one that has spawned a thousand imitations, recreations and debates over various aspects of its legality, but which remains a masterpiece, both of artistic attacking rugby, and

of commentary from Cliff Morgan. It came in the All Blacks fixture in 1973 against a Barbarians team that was, in all but name, a British & Irish Lions line-up. No matter how many times you watch footage of the try, it still has the ability to thrill. From Phil Bennett's jaw-dropping sidesteps, through John Dawes' burst up the left and Tom David's unlikely offload, to Derek Quinnell's final (forward?) pass. As so often, Edwards arrives on the scene as though in fast-forward mode, almost from off-stage in theatrical terms, moving at twice the speed as everyone else in picture, leaving All Blacks trailing behind him, ending the whole movement with a full-length dive into the corner. In Morgan's immortal, breathless words: 'This is Gareth Edwards! A dramatic start! What a score!' And who cares if there might have been a forward pass or two involved?

By now, Bennett had replaced Barry John as Edwards' half-back partner for Wales, and that would be the case on the Lions' tour to South Africa in 1974. The firmer grounds of South Africa would suit those dancing feet of Bennett, while Edwards, aged 27 at the start of the tour, was probably at his peak. Playing behind perhaps the greatest of all Lions forward packs, they would be a wonderfully effective and eye-catching combination on that tour. Even though he had been considered the best No9 in the game for some time, Edwards had not stopped striving to improve. His passing, for one thing, had been polished during long hours of carefully tailored practice. 'He may have been born with an abundance of the essential ingredients for success, but hard work turned him into the player of legend,' Mervyn Davies said. 'In his younger days, Gareth had a tendency to rely on the dive pass, but it was pointed out to him that as soon as he hit the deck he was out of the game. He spent hour after hour perfecting long, arrow-straight passes off both left and right hands.'

For all the expectation of hard grounds, downpours ensured that the first Test would be played in a bog at Newlands, Cape Town, making for a low-scoring, tryless contest. The Lions' pack were at their dominant best, Bennett kicked his goals and then Edwards produced a piece of magic to put the Lions out of sight. Just inside the Springboks' half, the Lions forwards secured possession and

recycled to Edwards. With a brief look up, he took a couple of steps to his right, took aim and launched an astonishing drop-goal from 40 metres. 'There was nothing on, no real danger to South Africa, on a particularly heavy part of the pitch,' Dick Milliken, the Lions centre, said. 'The genius dropped one of the most magnificent goals I have ever witnessed.'

With the first Test in the bag, the Lions braced themselves for an angry herd of Springboks desperate for revenge in Pretoria. This time, though, the pitch was firm and the Lions were able to play the rugby they had been so keen to showcase, scoring five wonderful tries and conceding none. The forwards were well on top, giving Edwards and Bennett the chance to paint some pictures behind them. The first try came from a solid scrum on halfway, from which Edwards picked up and launched a clever kick back over his shoulder. JJ Williams, on the left wing, had anticipated, but the Springboks were caught flat-footed and the Lions wing finished brilliantly for the first of his two tries on the day.

For Williams' second, the culmination of a stunning Lions counterattack started by Bennett,

Edwards added impetus in mid-movement before Williams popped up to finish. Bennett then scored a lovely individual try before Edwards caught a clearance kick from Ian McCallum, ran it back at pace and handed on for Gordon Brown to thunder over. The Springboks had been thumped, Edwards had produced another performance of the highest calibre and the Lions were on their way to another historic series win.

Just as the partnership with John had adorned the first half of Edwards' career, his pairing with Bennett continued to delight Welsh fans, bringing another grand slam in 1976 and enduring until the ends of their international careers. They did not know it at the time, but they were both to bow out after the final match of the 1978 Five Nations, when Wales would face France in Cardiff, both teams retaining a chance of the grand slam. Although France opened the scoring, Bennett jinked his way over beautifully for the first of his two tries before bursts from Edwards and JJ Williams created his second. Edwards' kicking, meanwhile, was sensational, including another of those off-the-cuff, perfectly struck snap drop-goals. Another grand

'He reached standards that were higher than anything I'd ever seen on a rugby field.'
– Phil Bennett

slam was completed and both half backs had taken their leave of the golden era with a suitable sense of style, Bennett incredibly grateful to have been granted a front-row seat to watch Edwards at work.

'He reached standards that were higher than anything I'd ever seen on a rugby field,' Bennett said. 'Gareth was voted by one rugby magazine as the greatest rugby player of all time and had there been any other result then I don't think I'd have been alone in demanding a recount. Other players have been more skilful, but in terms of overall attributes and the application of those in big matches year after year, I think he stands alone. He was never a one-man team, but he was the one man every other team would have killed for.'

Ian McLauchlan, the 'Mighty Mouse' who punched way above his weight on two victorious Lions tours in the 1970s

IAN MCLAUCHLAN

Name	Ian McLauchlan
Birthdate	14 April 1942
Birthplace	Tarbolton
Country	Scotland (43 caps)
Position	Loosehead prop – No1
Lions caps	8

He was not the biggest, nor the most dynamic, but McLauchlan made the most of everything he had to become a cornerstone of the Lions pack on those two famous tours of the early 1970s.

Whenever the 1971 British & Irish Lions tour to New Zealand is discussed, Ian McLauchlan has been known to bridle at the suggestion that he only played in the Test series because of the absence of others. In the week before the first Test, the Lions had lost two props to injury, Ray McLoughlin and Sandy Carmichael, in a brutally violent tour match against Canterbury. McLoughlin, of Ireland, was a formidable loosehead prop, McLauchlan's position, while Carmichael, a fellow Scot, was a tight-head. But McLauchlan felt he was always in with a good shot of starting in the No1 shirt in the

Test team, given his scrummaging ability and his mobility in the loose, which he felt was some way ahead of McLoughlin.

In the event, it was immaterial who would have started had both looseheads been available, because McLauchlan did not just start the first Test, he scored a crucial try and went on to play in all four Tests as the Lions recorded their only series victory in New Zealand. Three years later, in South Africa, he was once again ever-present in a Test team that remained unbeaten. On two iconic Lions tours, McLauchlan had started at loosehead in all eight Tests and, what is more, he

McLauchlan and Billy Steele train together before they made their debuts for Scotland against England at Twickenham in 1969. Both would go on to tour with the Lions

had lost only one of them. That is quite some record for a player who some had felt would be too small to take on the rugged packs of the southern hemisphere giants.

At 5ft 9in and 14st 7lb, the Scotland prop was never going to intimidate opponents with his size. He made up for that with his technique and sheer strength in the scrum, and the ferocity of his approach to the game around the park. If any opponent was tempted to underestimate him, they would soon discover an ability to punch well above his weight, sometimes,

as has often been said of him, all too literally. Hence the nickname of 'Mighty Mouse', which attached itself to him on that 1971 tour, and has remained with him ever since.

Between his two Lions tours, he took great pride in being chosen to lead Scotland, a role he would perform on 19 of the 43 occasions he played for his country, a record at the time. His ebullient character made him a natural leader, leading his troops into battle on the pitch, and willing to stand up for his players off the field. In the redoubtable Scottish pack of the 1970s, here was a prop who would never take a backward step, the sort of player around whom a pack could be built. As Phil Bennett, his teammate on the 1974 Lions tour said, succinctly: 'He was a hard man, was Mouse.'

It does not come as a surprise to many who took the field with McLauchlan that he was something of a boxer in his younger days. Growing up in Tarbolton, a village just outside Ayr, he was the son of a coal miner, Hugh, who was determined that his son would not follow him down the pit, a trait he shared with some of his Welsh teammates on those Lions tours. His father had seen local lads leaving school early and enjoying earning money in their teens, but McLauchlan's father was determined his son would finish his education and move onto other things. 'When Dad thought I could be tempted by the money, he showed me what a miner's life was like,' he has said. 'Darkness like you'd never believe, digging on your belly, it was inhuman. When we got back up, Dad said: "What do you think of that?" I said: "Horrible, never in my life will I go down there again." "Good," he said.'

The boxing steadily gave way to rugby, which he enjoyed more, and after school he attended teacher training college in Glasgow, and played much of his club rugby for Jordanhill, the team based at his college. He would go on to work as a PE teacher for 14 years before setting up a marketing and sponsorship business.

He was a month short of his 27th birthday by the time he won his first cap, against England at Twickenham in 1969. A competitive Scottish pack was just taking shape, with Carmichael packing down on the opposite side of the front row, Peter Brown and Alastair McHarg in the second row, and Jim Telfer at No8, but Scotland had not won at Twickenham since 1938 and it was

no different that year. For his second international, against South Africa at Murrayfield nine months later, he was joined by Gordon Brown, a fellow Ayrshire man making his debut, who would go on to play with him so successfully for the Lions, although their relationship was not so cordial at that point.

Rooming together in Edinburgh the night before the game, McLauchlan asked Brown whether he snored. Brown said that he thought he did. 'Well, do it tonight and I'll punch you in the face,' McLauchlan said. Brown was so scared of upsetting his new teammate, apparently, that he barely slept a wink before the big game the next day.

McLauchlan's first full Five Nations campaign, in 1971, was an eventful one. Scotland would lose to France and Ireland, and at Murrayfield they faced a Wales team who were establishing themselves as the tournament's dominant force, playing some of their finest rugby for years, but cruelly undone by a late try from Gerald Davies, converted from the touchline by John Taylor. Three defeats from three matches, extending their losing streak to five matches, and the final game was another visit to Twickenham.

In his first seven matches for Scotland, McLauchlan had finished on the winning side only once.

Midway through the second half, they looked to be heading for defeat once more, trailing England 15–5. But Duncan Paterson, the Scotland scrum half, dropped a goal and scored a try to bring them back into the contest at 15–11. With the clock ticking down, McLauchlan led the charge as Scotland sought to maintain their momentum. From a shortened lineout 30 metres from the English line, the prop stood at first receiver outside Paterson, and raced onto a short pass into the heart of the England pack inside the 22. The impact was immense, defenders scattering around him, and Scotland were on the front foot. To complement his potent scrummaging, this was what McLauchlan was capable of in the loose.

The ball was moved swiftly left, where Peter Brown's overhead pass found Chris Rea, who scored to bring Scotland to within a point. Brown then nervelessly converted and Scotland's comeback was complete, a 16–15 victory, their first at Twickenham for 33 years, a Five Nations whitewash averted in the most unlikely fashion. For good measure, a week later they beat England again, a one-off fixture arranged to commemorate 100 years since the first international match. It was a game England must have wished had never been arranged. They travelled to Murrayfield and were beaten 26–6. The foundations of a Scottish revival were being laid, built around the power and skill of their burgeoning forward pack.

Those performances helped five of that Scotland pack – McLauchlan, Carmichael, Frank Laidlaw, Gordon Brown and Rodger Arneil – to win selection for the Lions' tour to New Zealand that summer. The first challenge for McLauchlan, as it was for most players in the amateur days, was to work out how they could afford three months away from their jobs. His employer, Glasgow Council, would not grant him any more time off for rugby, so he sold his car, asked the bank to defer mortgage payments until he returned and his wife, Aileen, resolved to get a job to tide them over.

The Lions had been badly beaten in each of their two previous series in New Zealand, in 1959 and 1966, and when they were beaten by Queensland in Brisbane, one of two matches in Australia en route to New Zealand, the Kiwi public began to savour the prospect of some easy fodder for their cherished All Blacks. Once in New Zealand, however, they began to assert themselves and swept aside a string of provincial teams. It was becoming clear that the All Blacks would have a battle on their hands and the penultimate game before the Test series was against Canterbury in Christchurch. The Canterbury team had a track record of intimidating opponents and softening up the Lions before the Test, it seemed, was very much part of the plan.

That game would come to be known as one of the most notorious in Lions history. This was a time long before video referrals or even neutral referees and that day at Lancaster Park there was little protection for the players from the match officials. In the scrums, Carmichael was punched repeatedly in the face by his opposite number, Alister Hopkinson. At a lineout, he was elbowed in the eye. When he found himself caught at the back of a ruck, he was kicked in the other eye. Carmichael had to leave the field, both eyes swollen, gashed and almost closed.

It was not just Carmichael who suffered, as there were punch-ups all over the field. Fergus Slattery was concussed by a punch, while Gareth Edwards, the scrum half,

McLauchlan, in action here against England, relished the physical confrontations of the international game

was being attacked by Alex Wyllie, so Ray McLoughlin attempted to protect him, threw a punch at Wyllie, and broke his thumb in the process. Both Carmichael and McLoughlin were out of the rest of the tour. Carwyn James, the Lions coach, described the scene in the dressing room after the game. 'Like a casualty clearing station,' he said.

But the Lions won 14–3 and the fact that they had been prepared to stand up for themselves in the face of such naked aggression sent its own message to the New Zealanders.

McLauchlan (centre) keeps an eye on Malcolm Young, the England scrum half, in the drawn Five Nations match at Twickenham in 1979

'It was a bad game,' McLauchlan said. 'Rugby is like boxing, you don't need to go out and fight dirty, but if somebody is going to punch you, then you've got to lay into them. If you don't, they will keep punching you. It's like bullies all over the world. They knew if they punched me I would punch them back with no hesitation, so they didn't do it. The Test matches were as clean as any game you played in, hard but clean, and hard because they knew that if they started it, we'd finish it.'

For all that the Lions had stood up to those intimidatory tactics, they had still lost two prop forwards from the tour and the front row, therefore, was seen as a potential area of weakness going into the Test series. Others might have seen McLauchlan and Sean Lynch, the Irish tight-head, as second-string options, but

they were determined to prove they were up to the task. The first Test was in Dunedin, in front of 45,000, and although the All Blacks began playing at a fierce tempo, it was the Lions who scored first.

It was a statement score, too, because the try was scored by none other than McLauchlan. The movement began from a lineout on the right, where Delme Thomas won clean ball, which the Lions' backs moved swiftly left. John Bevan, the left winger, cut an aggressive line in off his wing and thundered into the New Zealand defence, spilling possession as he did so 20 yards from the line. The All Blacks shuffled the ball back to Alan Sutherland, the No8, who attempted a hasty clearing kick. McLauchlan had seen Sutherland shaping to kick, rushing over and extending himself to his full height, such as it was, to charge the kick down. The ball ran loose over the line, McLauchlan was the quickest to react and plunged on the ball to score.

He could not quite believe it at first, looking quizzically towards the referee to see whether he was giving a knock-on. But no, he was raising his arm to award the try; the Lions had drawn first blood in the series. It was the first try of McLauchlan's international career. It would also prove to be the only one he scored in a career of 51 internationals for Scotland and the Lions. What a time to score it. Mighty Mouse had announced himself to the All Blacks.

The All Blacks fought back furiously, surging forward in wave after wave of relentless attack, but the Lions' defence was unstinting too, tackling themselves almost to a standstill. The scrum was a further source of strength for the Lions and Barry John's boot kept nudging them ahead when given the chance, securing a priceless 10–3 victory. 'I don't know how many tackles I made that day, but it was a lot,' McLauchlan said. 'We were elated but on our knees, really tired. It was probably the most intense game of rugby I ever played in.'

In all four Tests of that series, McLauchlan was packing down against Brian 'Jazz' Muller, the All Blacks' tight-head who, at 6ft 1in and 17st 13lb, towered over his Scottish adversary at the set-piece. McLauchlan used his stature to his advantage, twisting his way under Muller, putting pressure on his neck, and generally making a nuisance of himself. Although the All Blacks won the second Test to level the series, the Lions' pack felt they had the measure of their opponents and ensured they could not lose the series with a 13–3 win in the third Test in Wellington, a dominant forward performance laying the foundation for tries from Gerald Davies and Barry John. The fourth Test was drawn and the Lions had sealed a historic series win. 'We knew we could easily hold them up front,' McLauchlan said. 'In the third Test their forward effort collapsed, we won it really easily and that killed them off.'

Back in Scotland, McLauchlan's enhanced status as one of the Lions who had won in New Zealand strengthened his standing and his leadership qualities. He was made captain for the first time before the Five Nations game in 1973 against Wales at Murrayfield and he immediately resolved to do the job his own way. It had long been a tradition for Scotland's home internationals that the president of the Scottish Rugby Union, along with the selectors, had been allowed into the team's dressing room before a game, up to and including the captain's pre-match pep talk.

McLauchlan had always felt uneasy about this, instinctively feeling that such moments should not be shared with outsiders, and he asked that the dignitaries leave before he delivered his speech. This was the amateur era, when the old men in blazers held considerable sway, and they left the dressing room only with the greatest reluctance. It was a controversial move and Alastair McHarg, the Scotland lock, said to McLauchlan: 'We're going to have to win this game now, otherwise you'll never play for Scotland again.'

Their opponents that day were the Wales team who had not lost a game in the Five Nations over the previous two seasons. But Scotland went out and played out of their skins, winning 10–9, scoring two tries of their own and preventing that multi-talented Welsh team from crossing the line. The decisive score came from a scrum near the Welsh line, with McLauchlan and Carmichael setting the most secure of platforms, Dougie Morgan passed out to Colin Telfer, who found a gap in Wales' defensive line to score.

It was a wonderful way to launch McLauchlan's captaincy and, at the very least, it ensured he would play for Scotland again. In fact, he would be captain for the next four years. 'I've heard players say that the pressure of captaincy affected them,' he said. 'It was the opposite for me, I was desperate to do it, I absolutely loved it.'

For the Lions' tour to South Africa in 1974, McLauchlan and Carmichael were selected in the squad again, along with their English counterparts, Fran Cotton and Mike Burton. They were considered a tough set of props and this was a particularly strong Lions squad, built around a core of players bringing with them the invaluable experience of winning against the All Blacks three years earlier. If that trip to New Zealand had been a strenuous test of heart and physicality, those who had been to South Africa before, such as Willie McBride, the captain, knew that this tour could be even more demanding. 'There's going to be a lot of intimidation, a lot of cheating,' he told his players before they set off. 'If you're not up for a fight, there's the door.'

One match early in the tour against Eastern Province was a brutal affair, with fights breaking out all over the field, but whenever the Lions were threatened with such violence, wise from their experience in New Zealand, they were sure to get their retaliation in first. As the Test series approached, they knew that a mighty forward tussle awaited, and placed huge emphasis in their preparation on ensuring their scrum would be a weapon. They would practise between 60 and 70 live scrums per day, eight against eight, with scrummaging machines yet to appear on the scene. The sessions were hugely competitive, but helped to forge a real bond among the pack. 'The forwards in '74, you didn't mess with those guys,' McBride said. 'Hell of a pack of forwards. I knew we had the men to stand up to anything that was going to be thrown at them.'

McLauchlan and Cotton were the starting props for all four Tests, packing down either side of Bobby Windsor, the Welsh hooker, a front row that gelled to telling effect. They ended the tour unbeaten, the forwards comprehensively winning the physical contest, the backs running in some thrilling

'I've heard players say that the pressure of captaincy affected them. It was the opposite for me. I absolutely loved it.'
– Ian McLauchlan

tries behind them. It was some achievement and McLauchlan was one of only five players to have featured in all eight Tests on those two momentous tours. 'I don't think overall 1974 was a better team, but the forward unit was better,' McLauchlan said. 'I really enjoyed the tour to South Africa. We had a great bunch of boys and it was much better being one of the senior players at that point.'

Rugby is a game of big men, of collisions and contests in which physical power and size is frequently the dominant factor, so when smaller players come along and prove their worth against bigger opponents, those are moments that spectators relish. Mighty Mouse McLauchlan was one such player, proving that guile, attitude, heart and technique – along with his own considerable strength – could be more than a match for the giant packs of the southern hemisphere.

Keith Wood, the livewire hooker, who produced some astonishing performances for the Lions in South Africa in 1997 and Australia in 2001

KEITH WOOD

Name	Keith Wood
Birthdate	27 January 1972
Birthplace	Killaloe
Country	Ireland (58 caps)
Position	Hooker – No2
Lions caps	5

As forthright and fierce as any front-rower, Wood was also blessed with a wide range of softer skills that made him a wonderfully rounded hooker.

There are certain things that hookers are supposed to do. With your arms around the props on either side, put your head down in the scrum, ensure that possession is secured and shove. Throw in at the lineouts. Around the field, make your tackles, hit the rucks and shovel the ball on when it comes your way.

There are certain things that hookers are not supposed to do. Stand out on the wing waiting for a cross-kick. Attempt a drop-goal in the dying seconds of an international match from near the halfway line. Sidestep your way over the tryline from 25 metres out. Even though he looked every inch the traditional hooker, with his rugged features, bald head and ursine physique, Keith Wood did all this and much more over the course of his international career.

He did the normal stuff as well, but there were matches when the casual observer might have wondered whether there were two bald hookers playing in either the green of Ireland or the red of the British & Irish Lions, so frequent were Wood's involvements. Along with the hard-nosed hooker's usual qualities, and a conspicuous twinkle in his eye, he brought an athleticism and appetite for the game that were far from familiar in a front-row forward. By the time he had

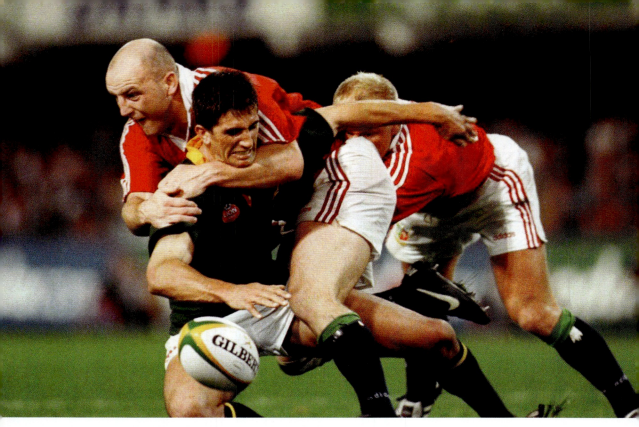

Wood and Neil Back tackle Henry Honiball during the Lions' series-clinching victory over the Springboks in Durban in 1997

hung up his boots, the mould of what was expected from a hooker had been well and truly broken.

In a career that straddled the game's move to professionalism, Wood won 58 caps for Ireland, 36 of them as captain. He was picked for two tours with the Lions, to South Africa in 1997 and Australia four years later, playing a starring role on each of them, both on and off the pitch. On the highly successful trip to South Africa, which did so much to broaden the Lions' appeal, he formed part of an unfancied Lions front row that disconcerted their mighty Springbok opponents.

Away from the game, as anyone who has watched the tour documentary *Living with Lions* will attest, he also performed a highly entertaining role as a wig-wearing judge in the post-match players' mock court sessions, delivering justice to Lions players who had strayed from the straight and narrow. The sentences handed down were often severe, alcohol-based punishments, and the court sessions were a central feature in contributing to the morale of the tour.

In Australia in 2001, the tour was not quite as harmonious or as successful on the field, but Wood was at his peak and turned in some outstanding performances. The series against the Wallabies ended in a defeat that was particularly galling, because the touring team had played some brilliant rugby in the series and came agonisingly close to winning, but Wood's place as one of the great Lions front-row forwards was secured.

Selection for the Lions is a special moment for any British and Irish player, but there was an extra layer of pride for Wood, as he was following in the footsteps of his father, Gordon. From 1954 to 1961, Gordon Wood won 29 caps as a prop for Ireland, to which he added two Test appearances for the Lions on their 1959 tour to New Zealand and Australia. He would not go on to see his son earning the same honours, though, as he died from a heart attack in 1982, aged 50. Keith was only 10 at the time.

In his youth, growing up in Killaloe, 15 miles north of Limerick, he played hurling and football as well as rugby. But the rugby was strong at his school, St Munchin's College, and after school he went to play for his father's old club, Garryowen, one of the powerhouses of the game in Munster. Much of his senior club rugby was played away from Ireland, joining Harlequins in England in 1995 as the game turned professional. He did return home for one season as a 'sabbatical' to play for Munster, his home province, who were such a gathering force at the time, as the game grew in Ireland around the success of provincial teams in the Heineken Cup. In Wood's season back in Limerick, they reached their first final, losing out narrowly to Northampton Saints, but Munster would become one of the most successful teams in Europe over the next decade.

Otherwise, his club career was spent at Harlequins, the well-to-do club in south-west London that might not have seemed the natural destination for a boy from Limerick, although, typically, that was part of the appeal for Wood. 'I liked the idea,' he said, glint in his eye, 'of this mad Irishman playing for the most English of clubs.'

His early appearances for Ireland were not the most straightforward of introductions to

A charismatic personality, who wore his heart on his sleeve, leadership roles came to him naturally.

the international scene. The mid-1990s were not a time of strength in Irish rugby and, having made his debut against Australia in 1994, aged 22, Wood then played in five successive Five Nations championships in which Ireland failed to win more than a single match. From 1996 to 1998, they landed the dreaded wooden spoon, finishing bottom of the pile. Lucky for them, it seemed at that stage, that Italy were about to join the competition.

In his first 17 matches for his national team, Ireland recorded only two victories, and those came against tier two rugby nations in United States and Japan. 'We didn't win regularly until the latter half of my career and it was sometimes really, really hard,' Wood said. 'But every chance I got to represent my country I thought it was just a magnificent thing to do.'

A charismatic personality, who wore his heart on his sleeve, leadership roles came to him naturally and Wood found himself captaining Ireland for the first time, against Australia in Dublin, in only his seventh Test. At a time when Ireland were losing so much more than they were winning, that was not an easy job to take on.

He had to battle his way through a number of injuries in those early days, too, to his shoulders in particular. Surgeries were necessary and when the shoulder went again he was being told by more than one doctor that, at the age of 23, retirement from rugby was a real possibility. But he sought further medical opinion and eventually met Ian Bayley, a surgeon in London, and realised that recovery was possible. Nevertheless, by the time he went on tour with the Lions to South Africa in 1997, he had been through two operations on his left shoulder and three on his right. The fact that Ian McGeechan, the head coach, was prepared to take him on tour, in spite of this injury record, showed just how much potential he recognised in the Ireland hooker.

The first Lions tour of the professional era was a watershed in more ways than one. For all the affection that the Lions concept had built up over the previous century, there were fears that it would be threatened by the move to professionalism, that the romantic notion of four international teams coming together as one every four years could soon be seen as an anachronism.

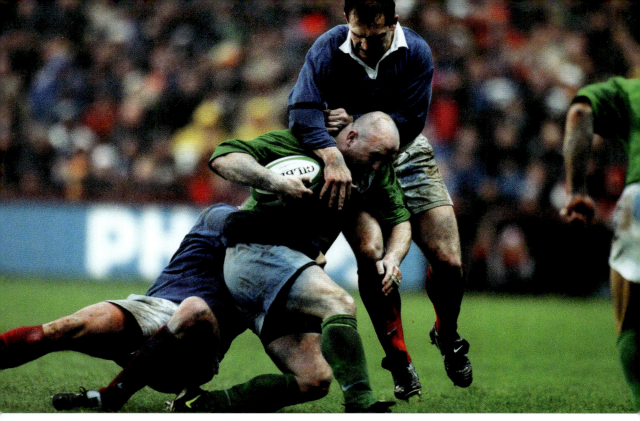

Wood caught in a double tackle by Richard Dourthe and Philippe Benetton for Ireland against France in the 1999 Five Nations

The Lions also went into the series against South Africa as colossal underdogs, as the Springboks had become world champions on home soil just two years earlier.

But the spirit that the squad developed on tour, to which Wood contributed more than his fair share, along with the success they consequently enjoyed in the Test series, showed that the Lions concept was, if anything, to be treasured even more in the professional era. Old-school values could sit alongside new-age preparation and form a heady mix in a touring team determined to honour some cherished traditions.

The Lions' status as underdogs had never looked more pronounced than in the front rows who squared up to each other for the first Test in Cape Town. By comparison, the Springboks were simply enormous. Os du Randt, the loosehead prop, was four stones heavier than Paul Wallace, the Lions prop he would be packing down against. On the other side of the scrum, Adrian Garvey towered over Tom Smith, while Naka Drotské, the hooker, was almost a stone heavier than Wood. In their customary fashion, the Springboks were determined to take the Lions on up front and outmuscle them at the set-piece.

But events did not quite unfold as expected. Turning a lack of height to their advantage, the Lions front row burrowed under their opponents in the scrum, using technical knowhow and an occasional resort to the dark arts, and the Springboks began to grow frustrated and penalties ensued. They were throwing everything at the Lions, but Neil Jenkins kept kicking the penalties to keep his team in touch. Late in the game, Matt Dawson scored an opportunist try, Alan Tait added another and the Lions had recorded an utterly unexpected win, all stemming from their refusal to be intimidated up front.

'There's a psychological impact on a team who know they're bigger and stronger and heavier and more powerful, but despite that they can't get in control of the scrum,' Wood said. 'The South Africans weren't destroying the opposition scrum and it became demoralising for them.'

If kicking was crucial in the first game, it became even more so in the second Test in Durban. It was a game that Lawrence Dallaglio, the England flanker, described as 'the most physical game I played in during my entire career'. The Springboks were determined to wreak revenge, and they battered away relentlessly at the Lions' defence, scoring three tries to none. What they failed to do was kick their goals, with no fewer than six shots at the posts – from three different kickers – going astray. Jenkins, meanwhile, slotted his chances metronomically and, despite being outplayed for large parts of the game, the Lions were hanging in there at 15–15, until two more kicks helped to decide the series.

Wood was an inspirational figure for Ireland, captaining in 26 of his 58 Tests for them

The more famous of the two was the drop-goal struck by Jeremy Guscott, which gave the Lions a lead that they would not lose. As well as holding his own in the physical stakes, taking on that formidable front row once again, who else contributed a crucial kick in those closing stages? None other than Keith Wood.

The Lions were running out of steam and their hooker had injured his ankle, but at a breakdown in his own half, Wood spotted the ball squirting out of the ruck, picked it up and instinctively kicked ahead. It was a brilliant kick, perfectly weighted, Wood chased 40 metres after it himself and forced the South Africans to concede a lineout in their own 22. 'The ball popped out and I just kicked it,' Wood said. 'And then I went, "Jesus, I have to run after it now".' Hookers just aren't supposed to do things like that.

From a position where they were clinging on for dear life, suddenly the Lions were on the attack. Wood then gathered his senses, caught his breath, threw accurately into the lineout to find Jeremy Davidson, and two phases later Guscott dropped the goal that would go down in Lions history. The series was won, the sense of elation was extraordinary.

'We were pretty much beaten up in both the games, those first two Tests, and yet we won both of them,' Wood said. 'For the last couple of seconds of that second Test, the sense of release and relief was pretty amazing. I tore my groin in the last minute of the game, so I was in agony. But it was happy agony.'

That tour to South Africa cemented Wood's reputation that he was growing into one of the finest hookers in the game and he went back desperate to lift Ireland's fortunes. The first international of the following season, though, was against New Zealand in Dublin, a side that Ireland had never beaten up to that point, and they were duly trounced 63–15 by a fine All Blacks team.

But Wood managed to shine nonetheless, scoring his first two international tries. The first was the sort that hookers are supposed to score. At a lineout near the All Blacks' line, Wood threw in to Malcolm O'Kelly, joined the back of the ensuing maul that drove forward and then flopped over the line. The second was the sort of try that hookers are not supposed to score. As Ireland attacked down the right and New Zealand scrambled to recover, Wood found himself in midfield on the New Zealand 22. Eric Miller, standing next to him, spotted space behind the defence, chipped over the top into the in-goal area and Wood set off in pursuit, pitting himself against Jeff Wilson.

Now Wilson was a winger, one of the best in the game, and although he had to turn, he had a head start on Wood. Incredibly, the Ireland captain surged past him and, as they both dived for the ball, it was Wood who reached out to touch down the bouncing ball. For a man of 6ft and nearly 17 stone, he had shown a remarkable turn of speed, the sort that hookers really aren't supposed to possess.

Against Wales the following season, a game played at Wembley while the Millennium Stadium was under construction, he popped up in the fly half position 25 metres from the Welsh line. What he was doing there was anybody's guess, but he ran onto the ball at pace, stepped nimbly off his left foot to leave Scott Gibbs flailing on his backside and crossed under the posts. An astonishing effort for a hooker.

Wood's try-scoring would become something of a habit, especially once Ireland's results began to pick up. At the 1999 World Cup, he scored four in a game against United States. The last of them saw him throw the ball in on the right and then, as Ireland worked the ball left, he remained out near the right-hand touchline. Play was moved swiftly back towards the right and Eric Elwood, the fly half, had little support outside him. He lofted a kick towards the corner, bouncing over the tryline, and there was Wood suddenly appearing to touch down. It really ought to have been an outside back out there, but there was Ireland's hooker, giving a passable impersonation of a winger instead. By the end of his career, he had racked up 15 tries in his 58 caps for Ireland, a record at the time for a front-five forward.

A second Lions tour came in 2001 to Australia, where the touring team were followed by a huge contingent of travelling fans, inspired by the heroics in South Africa in 1997, forming what became the 'Sea of Red' in the stands throughout the tour. Under the coaching of Graham Henry, the squad building up to the Test series was nowhere near as cohesive as it had been in 1997, but this was a powerful Lions squad. They were once again facing the world champions, but the Lions made a storming start to the series in the first Test in Brisbane.

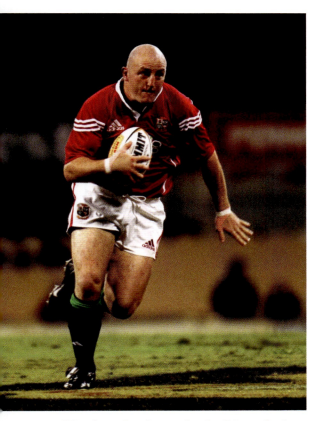

Wood on the charge for the Lions during the tour to Australia in 2001

Jason Robinson, fresh from his move to union from rugby league, scored a sizzling try in the third minute and the Lions were away, racing into a 12–3 lead by half-time, and extending it to an unthinkable 29–3 midway through the second half. Australia limited the damage with two late tries, but a 29–13 victory was a powerful statement by the Lions and the stars of the show had been two Irishmen, Brian O'Driscoll, who scored a wonderful try shortly after half-time, and Wood. Playing a full 80 minutes,

Wood was absolutely everywhere for the duration of the game, making ground with ball in hand, tackling hard, hitting rucks, scrummaging and, yes, kicking again.

When Stuart Barnes, commentating on television, made Wood his man of the match, the praise could not have been higher. 'I've never seen a hooker cover so much ground, make so many tackles, kick so well,' Barnes said. 'Tonight, he is a Lions legend.'

To put a final flourish on his performance, in the final minute Wood even attempted a drop-goal from 42 metres out. There he was again, doing things that hookers weren't supposed to do. It fell a good 10 metres short, but he had followed it up, made the tackle on Dan Herbert, and helped the Lions to close out the game. This was an individual performance for the ages in an outstanding team effort.

On that tour, though, it was not to last. The Wallabies fought back with a comprehensive 35–14 win in the second Test in Melbourne and injuries began to mount for the Lions, and they were running on fumes by the time of the deciding third Test. It was an exhilarating contest, the lead swinging back and forth, and with Australia leading

A textbook tackle from Wood on Serge Betsen of France during the 2003 World Cup quarter-final in Melbourne

29–23 in the closing stages, the Lions had one last chance to win the series with an attacking lineout 20 metres from the Wallabies' line. Wood wanted to throw to the back, Martin Johnson, the captain, wanted it thrown to the front. With two minutes remaining,

the hooker followed his captain's order, threw towards Johnson at the front, but Justin Harrison, the Australia lock, soared to claim the lineout steal of his life. 'I threw a pretty good throw, but they read it,' Wood said. 'But it didn't just come down to that. We were like the walking wounded at the end, I was unbelievably shattered.'

His last Lions involvement was a disappointing one, but once again Wood returned from tour with a mission to lift Ireland's performances to the next level. With the likes of O'Driscoll, Ronan O'Gara, Shane Horgan and Anthony Foley coming to the fore, they took a huge stride forward in the autumn of 2001. The conclusion to that year's Six Nations championship had been delayed – by the outbreak of foot-and-mouth disease – to the start of the 2001–02 season and it reached a climax when England visited Dublin needing one more victory to complete a grand slam. England had been dominant throughout the tournament, but Ireland were gathering momentum and the Lansdowne Road crowd were longing to spoil England's party.

Ireland were outstanding that day and Wood raised the roof when he scored their only try, a ferociously powerful effort that summed up everything he brought to the game. Ten metres from the English line, Wood threw into a lineout, where Mick Galwey caught and swiftly transferred to Foley at the back of the maul. Rather than driving the maul, Foley popped up a pass to Wood,

He was utterly unstoppable, scoring a try that will live long in the memory of every Irish supporter watching that day.

who had sprinted straight from taking the throw to run onto the ball.

By the time he ran round the side of the Irish maul, he was at full steam, and crashed through several English tacklers to plunge over the line. He was utterly unstoppable, scoring a try that will live long in the memory of every Irish supporter watching that day. They were not used to seeing hookers score tries like that. A few weeks later, he was named World Rugby's player of the year, and remains the only front-row forward to win the award. The expectations of what would be required from a hooker at international level had been changed for good.

Tadhg Furlong, the multi-skilled prop, who started every Test for the Lions in New Zealand in 2017 and South Africa four years later

Tadhg Furlong

Name	Tadhg Furlong
Birthdate	14 November 1992
Birthplace	Wexford
Country	Ireland (72 caps)
Position	Tight-head prop – No3
Lions caps	6

One of a glut of world-class players who elevated Irish rugby to new heights, Furlong raised the bar for the way tight-head props could influence a game around the field.

At first glance, when you watch Tadhg Furlong running out from the tunnel onto the field, he looks every inch the stereotype of a farmer-prop: square shoulders, huge barrel chest, rugged features. If anyone watching was previously unaware that the big bloke wearing No3 was from a farming background, they would probably guess it anyway. Across different countries and hemispheres, rugby union often has strongholds within agricultural communities – the Scottish borders, the south-west regions of both England and France, much of New Zealand – and the players traditionally produced are tough, gnarled, hardy forwards, more than capable of looking after themselves amid the close-quarter battles of the ruck, maul and scrum, blessed with almost mythical farmer-strength to guarantee a supply of possession for their team.

Packing down at tight-head prop for Ireland, Furlong fits the bill on all these counts, as befits his upbringing on a dairy farm in County Wexford. But watch him in action for a full match and you soon see that there is much more to his game than first meets the eye. As the professional era has progressed, the demands of prop forwards have continued to grow. Few can now get away with simply shoving in the scrum and lifting at the lineout. At international

Furlong, a farmer's son from Wexford, before the Lions' tour to New Zealand in 2017

level, it is now common for props to be able to carry, to handle and to make their share of tackles, but the skillset that Furlong brings to his position has lifted the business of propping to a whole new level. Along with the power-based elements of his game, there is a twinkletoed sidestep, deft distribution and an ability either to burst through tackles or to offload if he is held.

He has been a cornerstone of the most successful era Irish rugby has known, featuring two Six Nations grand slams in six seasons, four victories over New Zealand, including a series win away from home, and long spells as the number one ranked team in the world. There have been trophies aplenty with Leinster, the province that provides so many players to Ireland, and he became the natural choice as starting tight-head on two tours with the British & Irish Lions, first in the compelling series in New Zealand in 2017, which ended in a dramatic draw, and then in South Africa four years later, where the Lions suffered a narrow series defeat. As he was only 28 when that series against the Springboks concluded, the possibility of appearing in a third series remains.

Representing the Lions was the fulfilment of a childhood dream for Furlong, because, as an eight-year-old, he had spent the summer of 2001 wearing a replica red shirt and watching the Lions' series in Australia. Growing up in Campile, a village east of Waterford, his father, James, had been a prop for the local club, New Ross, and began coaching junior rugby when his playing days had ended. Tadhg would milk cows on the family farm from the age of four or five, and began playing rugby at a similar time.

While rugby kept him occupied in the winters, he would play Gaelic football in the summer, employing the same approach he brought to his rugby, relishing the physical contests and proving surprisingly mobile for his size. Although he was clearly a talented player, he was not sure quite how good he was in comparison with the best of his age, because the pathways towards the professional game in Ireland tend to be split into two: club junior sections and private schools. Furlong came up through his club, he knew that schools players would have had access to the best coaching and facilities, and it was only when he was chosen for Ireland's Under 18 team that he was given the chance to measure himself up against the private school boys, and realised he

could cope. An academy contract with Leinster would follow and that would mean leaving home and moving two hours north to Dublin, the country boy relocating to the big city. 'My first night up in Dublin,' he said, 'I was ringing up my mother asking how to cook pasta.'

He learned the cooking soon enough and was fortunate in his early days at Leinster to be educated in the finer points of scrummaging by Mike Ross, Ireland's longstanding tight-head prop. He graduated from the academy to a senior contract with Leinster, becoming the first player from his part of County Wexford to make the grade as a professional. The pupil would soon take the place of his mentor, both for province and country, because at the end of Furlong's first season in the full Leinster squad he was given an international debut, aged 22, in a warm-up match for the 2015 World Cup against Wales.

His first start at international level came the following summer, on tour to South Africa, and it was a daunting

He has been a cornerstone of the most successful era Irish rugby has known.

one, packing down opposite 'The Beast', Tendai Mtawarira, the Springboks' legendary loosehead, and acquitting himself well. His next start would be another huge challenge, wearing the No3 shirt for Ireland's gospel-spreading match against New Zealand in Chicago.

This was a momentous time to be breaking into the national team. Under the coaching of Joe Schmidt, Ireland had won back-to-back Six Nations titles in 2014 and 2015, and a generation of bright young talents were making their way through, ready to replace the likes of Paul O'Connell, Brian O'Driscoll and Gordon D'Arcy, legends who had served their country so well for so long. In Chicago that November day, the new generation played their part in an achievement unique in Irish rugby, their first ever victory over the All Blacks. They had been trying for 111 years and now they finally managed it.

The mistake they made was to have arranged another fixture against the same opponents two weeks later in Dublin. Smarting from their defeat in Chicago, the All Blacks came to Aviva Stadium and, somewhat inevitably, exacted a measure of revenge with a 21–9 victory. But Ireland were in the contest for most of the game and Furlong, in particular, showed the damage he was capable of doing with ball in hand. Early in the first half, taking a pass from Johnny Sexton near the halfway line, Furlong was slightly isolated, with two All Blacks bearing down on him. Not just any All Blacks, either, but Owen Franks, the mighty tight-head prop, and Brodie Retallick, the 6ft 8in behemoth of a lock.

Furlong first wrestled with Franks and shook him off, leaving him lying prone on the floor. Retallick had a go next and was shrugged aside with a massive right-arm fend that shoved him onto his backside. Then came Kieran Read and he fared no better, simply bumped backwards as he attempted to make the tackle. It took three more All Blacks finally to bring Furlong down. It was an astonishing display of power, marking out in no uncertain terms that Ireland's new tight-head prop, making only his second international start, was already capable of taking on the best in the world.

That performance against New Zealand and another impressive display against Australia the following week prompted talk of potential selection for the Lions at the end of that season. Just

Furlong makes ground during the Lions' victory over the Crusaders in the tour match in Christchurch in 2017

turned 24, with only a handful of international starts behind him, and none in the Six Nations, Furlong felt that any such talk was wildly premature, in typically self-effacing fashion. 'You get kind of embarrassed,' he said. 'I've only started four games for Ireland, had two Heineken Cup games for Leinster and it's a big, big step to be making those shouts. I think I have a long journey to go.'

As it turned out, the journey was not that long at all. He fared well in the scrum during his first full Six Nations championship, which culminated for Ireland in a joyous victory over England in Dublin, denying their opponents a grand slam. Furlong had done enough

to earn selection from Warren Gatland, the head coach, for the Lions' tour to New Zealand, one of three tight-head props along with Kyle Sinckler and Dan Cole, both of England. Time for another meeting with the All Blacks. Unusually for a British or Irish player, of his first 13 international starts, eight would come against the Big Three from the southern hemisphere: New Zealand, Australia and South Africa. A baptism of fire to some; for Furlong it merely gave a chance to prove his quality early in his career.

After encouraging performances in the early tour games, Furlong was chosen in the No3 shirt for the first Test in Auckland and, although the Lions competed

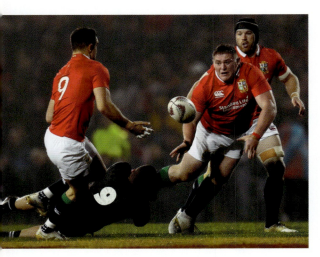

Blessed with outstanding handling skills, Furlong gets his offload away to Conor Murray for the Lions against the Maori All Blacks in 2017

well for much of the game, the All Blacks pressed the accelerator in the second half and ran out 30–15 winners. The second Test, in Wellington, was the day the Lions roared back into the series and succeeded not only in maintaining interest to the final match, but in underlining the value of the Lions concept. On the previous visit to New Zealand, in 2005, the Lions had been whitewashed in the series and changes made by Clive Woodward, the head coach, had proved hugely unpopular.

Furlong began the second Test with a bang. Taking a pass from Taulupe Faletau on the All Blacks' 22, he was confronted immediately by Jerome Kaino, the tough-as-teak blindside flanker. He initially rode the

challenge, then spun off. Kaino clung on with two arms, but now found himself being dragged backwards towards the goalposts. By the time he eventually brought Furlong to ground, the Irishman had made a good 10 yards in a crucial area of the pitch. These are the so-called hard yards, which put the opposition on the back foot, and Furlong had made them against a hard man, a statement of intent for the Lions that day.

They went on to win that Test, making the most of a red card for Sonny Bill Williams, the All Blacks' centre, and a 24–21 victory, scoring two tries to none, sent the series to a decider back in Auckland, to the sheer delight of the vast number of travelling Lions fans, the Sea of Red established once again. By now, those fans had taken Furlong firmly into their affections, his visibly wholehearted efforts in attack and defence raucously greeted from the stands, and he had even been granted his own song. To the tune of 'Que Sera, Sera', they sang:

'Tadhg Furlong, Furlong,
He's big and he's mighty strong,
He's right at the heart of the scrum,
Tadhg Furlong, Furlong.'

The New Zealand press, meanwhile, notoriously hard to please, were also clearly impressed, dubbing him the Sherman Tank for the strength of his carries and the difficulty the All Blacks were finding in putting him down.

This was an All Blacks team who had won the World Cup two years earlier and, of course, had only lost one series to the Lions in their history, against the team of 1971. That victory in the second Test ended a remarkable 47-match winning streak on home soil. So the third Test was an epic occasion, as the two packs went toe-to-toe. Furlong gave a good account of himself for an hour and was then replaced by Sinckler, which had proved a highly effective combination. In the end, the two teams could not be separated, the Test and the series were drawn. Make no mistake, though, this was a huge achievement for the Lions, as there had been doubts whether a team put together in such a short space of time could compete with the world champions on their home soil. They might have drawn the series, but this was a triumphant tour for the Lions.

Back with Ireland, Furlong was playing under a coach, Joe Schmidt, who was constantly working with his players to add new elements to their game. Furlong was already a rounded package, a force at the set-piece and

contributing far more around the field than most tight-head props. But Schmidt had also noticed how well Furlong handled the ball and thought that he could perhaps bring a little more of that to his game.

The next season's Six Nations saw Ireland chasing a grand slam, something they had achieved only twice before. They had come close plenty of times, but only in 1948 and 2009 had they managed to finish it off. In 2018, they would have to travel to Twickenham to complete the job, taking on an England team who had won the Six Nations title in each of the previous two seasons. The game fell on St Patrick's Day, a day of celebration for Irish folk whatever the result.

It was under these circumstances that Furlong's new role as a playmaker was seen to greatest effect. This was not just the case of occasional pieces of smart handling, he was now being entrusted with standing at first or second receiver, taking the place of the fly half, and distributing to set Ireland's attack in motion. In the 24th minute, he was standing out of an Ireland lineout, remaining in midfield instead. When the second pass came to him, using Sexton as a decoy, he swivelled instead, using his broad torso to shield the ball, and gave the most delicate of passes to send Bundee Aki through a hole. England's defence scrambled to recover, but Aki handed on to CJ Stander, who scored by the posts. Ireland were 14–0 ahead, a lead that they would not relinquish, and the third grand slam in their history was secure. Furlong was named man of the match – he had done the nuts and bolts of a prop forward's job pretty well, too – and the attacking variety of Ireland's game was being greatly enhanced by having ballplayers in so many different positions.

He is a try-scorer, too, crossing for the first time for Ireland on their successful summer tour to Australia after clinching the grand slam. After losing the first Test in Brisbane, the second match in Melbourne was in the balance early in the second half when Furlong's vision earned him a crucial score. At a ruck five metres from the Wallabies' line, Furlong was standing to the right of the breakdown with support, when he spotted chinks in defence to the other side of the ruck. Earlier in his career, he might have stayed where he was, but now he timed his movement behind the ruck, yelled to Conor Murray for the pass,

Furlong in action against Scotland in 2018, the fourth of five wins that clinched Ireland a Six Nations grand slam

and then barged his way between two defenders. This score, and the way he went about it, Furlong said afterwards, was a sign of his growing confidence in his abilities.

There were further tries to enjoy at the 2019 World Cup in Japan. Although Ireland again fell short at the quarter-final stage, Furlong was a conspicuous presence throughout the pool stages, scoring a barnstorming try against Samoa, when he ran onto a pass from Conor Murray 10 metres out, picking his line so that he smashed between the first two Samoan defenders, then had two more hanging off him for the last five metres before he reached over to score.

There would be fewer attacking opportunities on his second Lions tour, to South Africa in 2021. This was a dour, attritional series, in which the Lions' forwards were tasked with defusing the Springboks' famous 'Bomb Squad', the heavy-duty forward pack that had led them to World Cup success two years earlier. The series began well, with the Lions winning the first Test in Cape Town (where all three Tests would be held, due to Covid), their try coming from a masterful rolling maul, with Furlong at the heart of it, and Luke Cowan-Dickie touching down.

This was more a series for mauling and scrumming than running free in open space. The Lions were well beaten in the second Test and edged out in the third, but the front row, and Furlong in particular, had held their own against illustrious opponents. Covid restrictions meant that the stands were empty, a bizarre spectacle, which meant that there was no rendition of Furlong's personal song from four years earlier, at least not in the stadium. There will have been a few singing along while watching on television and there was no doubt that, over the course of two highly demanding tours, Furlong had proved his status as a genuine Lions great.

Such a suggestion would embarrass the man himself, of

> Over the course of two highly demanding tours, Furlong had proved his status as a genuine Lions great.

course. He seemed somewhat bashful, too, when he was asked to captain Ireland in 2022 against Fiji. In his pre-match media conference, he was asked whether leading his country was something he had dreamed about as a child. As the self-effacing type, he had clearly never expected such an honour to come his way. If not the Ireland captaincy, what did you dream of when you were younger? 'Spuds. Gravy. The mother's Sunday roast,' came the answer, a twinkle in his eye. And then, more seriously, a recognition of how far he had come, from his days on the family farm and at the local club in Wexford, to playing twice for the Lions and captaining Ireland. 'It's class, I know people from back home,' he said, 'and they'll be very proud.'

Maro Itoje, the all-action lock, who came of age on the Lions' tour to New Zealand in 2017

MARO ITOJE

Name	Maro Itoje
Birthdate	28 October 1994
Birthplace	Camden
Country	England (76 caps)
Position	Lock – No4
Lions caps	6

Some players have an ability to raise their game to meet the occasion. For England, Itoje's habitual standard of play was something special, but he raised his game to another level in a Lions shirt.

For those few rugby players lucky enough to become known as legends of the British & Irish Lions, the achievement is usually the culmination of a career in the game. It can take long years of striving for recognition with club and then country, adjusting to the pace of international rugby, learning how to win Test matches for your country, performing consistently against the best players in the world, and only then comes the possibility of another step up to become a Lion and the chance to shine on one of the game's grandest stages. Well, Maro Itoje had done all that by the age of 22.

He was the youngest player in the 41-man squad chosen by Warren Gatland, the head coach, for the series against New Zealand in 2017, but he came away as the tour's biggest star. Jonathan Davies, the Wales centre, was named man of the series after the Lions had scrapped their way to an epic 1–1 draw, with the deciding contest drawn, but Itoje, the England lock, had been the darling of the massed ranks of travelling red-shirted fans, going toe-to-toe with the world champion All Blacks and showing he could outperform them in their own back yard. 'Oh, Maro Itoje', the song sung throughout the series to the tune of

Itoje clings on during the Lions' tour match against the Maori All Blacks in 2017

'Seven Nation Army' by Lions fans, was the soundtrack to the tour. All that coupled with the frightening prospect, from an opponent's point of view, that he could only get better.

By the time he was 26, Itoje had been on a second Lions tour, to South Africa in 2021, he was again outstanding against world champion opponents, and this time he was named player of the tour. There was not the same acclaim from the stands this time, as the three Tests were played behind closed doors in Cape Town due to Covid restrictions, but Itoje had demonstrated a maturity to go with the all-round athleticism and power that he had displayed

in New Zealand four years earlier. His status as a world-class player did not need underlining, but he had done so anyway, reinforcing his place among the finest locks to have played for England and the Lions. Once again, to perform to such a level when he was still in his mid-twenties prompted the question of how much he might go on to achieve in the game. 'He climbed Everest as a young player,' Eddie Jones, the England head coach, said at the time. 'And it looks like he's going to climb another Everest as a mature player.'

However gifted the player, individual brilliance in rugby does not always translate into success that can be weighed in silverware, so dependent is each player on the collective performance. Some unquestionably great players can go a whole career without winning a significant trophy, but that has certainly not been the case with Itoje. Before he made it into the senior ranks, he had captained England to the World Under 20 title and in his first five seasons in club rugby with Saracens he won four Premiership titles and three Heineken Cups. At international level, in each of his first two seasons England won the Six Nations title. Clearly Itoje's presence contributed in no small way to these triumphs, but there was no doubt that his rich talent was nurtured in some flourishing environments at an early stage in his career.

Itoje was born and raised in north London, one of three children of Nigerian parents who moved to the UK in their twenties. His parents ran a butcher's shop initially before his father, Efe, became a consultant in the oil industry and his mother, Florence, became a property trader. They impressed on their children the value of education and Itoje first went to secondary school at St George's in Harpenden, a state school where he boarded, and where

Owen Farrell, later a teammate with Saracens, England and the Lions, was three years ahead of him. At the age of 16, he won a scholarship to Harrow School, one of the most prestigious schools in England. When he was offered a professional contract after leaving school by Saracens, his nearest professional club, his parents allowed him to accept it only on the understanding that he would also go to university.

As a result, in those first few years of his career, when he built such a reputation and won so many trophies, he was also studying for a politics degree at the School of Oriental and African Studies in London. His Nigerian heritage means a great deal to him and he would spend time there in summer holidays as a child, and has subsequently set up a charitable fund to provide education for disadvantaged children in Lagos, the capital. His breadth of interests have always marked him apart from the archetypal professional sportsman and there will be a fascination in the direction he takes once his playing days are done. 'I try not to be identified exclusively as a rugby player,' he said. 'I'm interested in politics, I'm interested in business, I'm interested in charities and art. I would want to keep a connection to rugby, but I won't be a coach and I wouldn't want to be a pundit. But rugby will always be the most important thing for however long I play.'

From his time in junior rugby, and particularly his efforts in leading his country to victory in the Under 20 World Championship final against South Africa in 2014, there was an expectation in English rugby that a potentially special player was on his way. His first full season with Saracens, including an impressive performance in the Premiership final victory over Bath, did nothing to quell the excitement and, at the age of 20, he was included in a wider England training squad for the 2015 World Cup on home soil.

He did not make the final cut, but when Eddie Jones replaced Stuart Lancaster in charge of England after the World Cup, the new coach quickly judged that Itoje was ready for the step up to international level, although he stressed that the youngster was far from the finished article. To illustrate his point, Jones said that he wanted to see Itoje become a BMW, rather than the Vauxhall Viva he resembled at the time.

Itoje had to use Google to understand Jones' reference to an obscure car from the 1970s, but his international debut came as a second-half replacement against Italy at Twickenham and he did not waste any time. One of his first acts was to soar in the lineout and pilfer possession from Sergio Parisse, the great No8, and an action-packed 25-minute cameo saw him promoted to the starting line-up for the rest of the Six Nations championship. In his second start, against Wales at Twickenham, he began to show the wider world what all the English hype over his arrival on the scene was about.

Starting in the second row alongside George Kruis, a partnership that would prove harmonious for both Saracens and England, Itoje produced a remarkably influential performance for one so new to international rugby. There are lock forwards who go about their business quietly and highly effectively without ever attracting the attention of the casual spectator, but Itoje, at 6ft 5in and with braided hair, has always caught the eye. He had always been comfortable during his junior days, playing either lock or blindside flanker, and against

Wales he seemed to do both jobs at once. He was England's most industrious defender, making 16 tackles and missing none, disrupting Welsh attacks at the breakdown and pinching two key lineouts on opposition ball. As the cherry on the cake, he made the run that set up England's only try in a 25–21 victory. Taking a pass 40 metres out on the left, he faded outside the challenge of Dan Biggar, the Wales fly half, who was advancing quickly, then powered through an attempted tackle from Scott Baldwin. With Alex Cuthbert clinging desperately onto his coattails, Itoje slipped out a lovely pass to Mike Brown, who put Anthony Watson into the corner. This was a highly accomplished display, winning him the man of the match award, earning Itoje grudging praise from his coach. 'He's a BMW now,' Jones said.

But there was a postscript to that Wales match. Despite the win for England against a team that had knocked them out in the World Cup, and his own all-round excellence, at the final whistle Itoje could be seen ripping off his scrum cap and throwing it to the ground in frustration. He was not happy. 'The last 10 minutes wasn't good enough, we were pretty poor,'

Itoje leads the Lions off after their epic victory over the All Blacks in the second Test in Wellington

he explained later. 'You want an 80-minute performance in every Test you play.' An indication, if ever there was, of a man demanding the highest standards of himself and his team.

The following weekend, in the first season of Jones' stewardship, England completed the grand slam, their first since 2003, the year they went on to win the World Cup. And the suggestion that something special might be brewing gained further credence when England went to Australia that summer and won the Test series 3–0, the first time they had won an away series against the Wallabies. In the 2017 Six Nations, they won their first four matches, missing out on a grand slam with a narrow defeat to Ireland in Dublin, but won the title for the second successive year. Throughout that tournament, Itoje played at blindside

Itoje carries hard during the series decider behind closed doors against South Africa in 2021

flanker, and his ability to play at either lock or No6 was an added attraction at this stage of his career, although he would ultimately settle to play the vast majority of international games in the second row.

The progress of Jones' side meant that, when Warren Gatland picked his British & Irish Lions squad to travel to New Zealand, England provided 16 members of the 41-man squad, comfortably the largest contingent, and Itoje was among them. As the youngest player, according to Lions tradition, he was entrusted with looking after the team's mascot, Bil, a cuddly Lion.

The second row looked an area of strength for the Lions and competition for Test places would

be stiff, with Kruis and Courtney Lawes from England in the squad, along with Iain Henderson from Ireland and Alun Wyn Jones, of Wales, who was on his third Lions tour and had captained them to victory in the deciding Test in Australia four years earlier.

For the opening Test in Auckland, Itoje was widely expected to start, after a series of fine performances in tour matches, including a try-scoring effort against Maori All Blacks, but Gatland went instead for Kruis, an expert lineout operator, to start alongside Jones, with Itoje among the replacements. The Lions were well beaten at Eden Park, but Itoje came off the bench to play 33 minutes and made a significant impact, prompting Gatland to call him into the starting line-up for the second Test in place of Kruis. A much-improved version of the Lions forward pack was in evidence in Wellington, even before they gained an advantage through the sending off of Sonny Bill Williams, the New Zealand centre, for a shoulder charge on Anthony Watson. Itoje was at his disruptive best, reaching for the All Blacks' lineout ball with his huge wingspan, stooping to slow their possession down at the rucks, tackling like a demon. His every involvement was serenaded by the fans – '*Oh, Maro Itoje*', on repeat – and the acoustics at the 'Cake Tin' stadium made it sound like a home fixture for the Lions. They went on to record their first win in New Zealand for 24 years and the series, thrillingly, would go to a deciding Test.

From the opening stages of that third Test in Auckland, Itoje had his fingerprints all over the game. An early New Zealand maul was scuppered by his telescopic left arm and that song was now ringing out around the Eden Park crowd, Itoje's father among them. On a wet day, he carried strongly, proved a constant nuisance at the rucks and soared high on the Lions' own lineout ball. It was, perhaps, his finest international performance to date, summoned against the best side in the world, his partnership with Jones integral to a successful tour. 'It's been nice to work with him,' Jones said with a smile. The third Test and the series were drawn, but the Lions could be delighted with their efforts. Brodie Retallick, the 6ft 8in All Blacks lock, had generally been considered to be the world's best second-row forward for the previous few years. Now Itoje

had gone toe-to-toe with him and looked every inch his equal. And remember, he was still only 22.

The progress England had made in Itoje's first two years in the side began to slow a little, with under-par performances in the Six Nations and a 2–1 series defeat in South Africa, but they were still among the favourites for a decent run at the World Cup in Japan in 2019. Although he was still only 24, with 29 caps to his name, Itoje's status since the Lions tour was such that he was now being considered a senior player. Through the pool stages, England were building momentum steadily and then they went up a couple of gears with an excellent showing in a quarter-final victory over Australia.

In the semi-final in Yokohama, Itoje would come face to face once more with the All Blacks, favourites for the tournament and still largely the team against whom he had excelled for the Lions. While England had been steadily improving, the quality of their performance in the semi-final was on another level altogether, especially in defence. From the moment that Manu Tuilagi opened the scoring with a try in the second minute, England were ferociously clinical with ball in hand,

and utterly voracious whenever New Zealand had possession.

This was undoubtedly the finest defensive performance in England's history and Itoje was right at the heart of it. He tackled black shirts in every way imaginable: Retallick was wrapped up in a huge bear hug of a smother tackle; Sonny Bill Williams was lassoed around the knees; Sam Whitelock was hit hard in the stomach as he caught the ball and driven yards backwards; Codie Taylor saw the ball ripped from his grasp. Itoje was an irresistible force. Rising in front of Kieran Read, he stole New Zealand's lineout ball. When the All Blacks mauled, Itoje's arm stayed in the middle to disrupt their ball, and when the maul collapsed, he somehow stayed on his feet to regain possession. When Beauden Barrett was caught 10 metres from his own line, Itoje latched onto him like a limpet to earn a penalty. His prowess at the breakdown had become a real super-strength, able to bend incredibly low for a man of his height, his muscular frame almost impossible for opponents to shift.

Sadly, in the final against South Africa, England were unable to rise to such heights again. The Springboks got on top of England's scrum from early

in the game and, having been shunted onto the back foot, it was a struggle for the forwards to regain dominance. England had peaked a week too early, South Africa were world champions for a third time.

A chance to exact some measure of revenge came for those England players selected for the British & Irish Lions trip to South Africa in 2021. There were 11 of them in a squad of 37, embarking on a Lions tour with a difference. The Covid pandemic meant that every match on tour would be played without fans, which gave the Test series, in particular, an eerie quality and made the tour as a whole, inevitably, much less enjoyable for the players. Yet the Test matches were still fought with huge intensity, even if there was a limited amount of attacking rugby on display.

Itoje had been one of the leading contenders to captain the Lions, although Gatland eventually plumped for his old second-row partner, Alun Wyn Jones, and they reprised their pairing from four years before. But Itoje also went to South Africa with something of a point to prove: although he had become widely recognised as one of the best players in the world, he had yet to produce his best against the Springboks. In Eben Etzebeth, they had their own candidate to be considered the best lock in the world and his match-up with Itoje would be eagerly awaited.

In the first Test, there was a clear winner of their contest, and South African fans, if they had been in any doubt, now understood what all the fuss was about. This was another one of those performances where Itoje seemed able to operate at a level of relentless intensity beyond any other player on the field. He thundered into Etzebeth with a dominant tackle early in the game, then bumped Kwagga Smith, the No8, to the floor before poaching possession from him. Grand larceny, some would say. He kept going for 80 minutes and, with the Lions leading 22–17 in the closing stages, Itoje, astonishingly, made no fewer than four crucial tackles in the final 70 seconds. At the end of such a lung-busting performance, those final efforts simply beggared belief.

'I said to the players that I get incredibly excited about these big games, because I love seeing the desire of the top players, how much they want to win these big matches,' Gatland said the day after. 'I saw that in Maro Itoje last night. His performance was outstanding.'

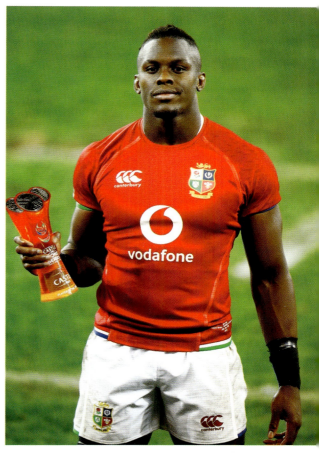

Itoje with the man of the match award after the Lions had won the first Test in South Africa in 2021

So often with Itoje that was the case on those showpiece occasions, for the Lions in particular. The next two Tests were lost, the third by an agonising 19–16 margin, but Itoje was named the Lions' player of the series. With two tours behind him, at the age of 26, he could look forward to the possibility of a third series in Australia in 2025, this time with the sea of red-shirted fans back in the stands.

Willie John McBride leads his Ireland team out before the victory over England at
Twickenham that would set them on the way to the 1974 Five Nations title

WILLIE JOHN MCBRIDE

Name	Willie John McBride
Birthdate	6 June 1940
Birthplace	Toomebridge
Country	Ireland (63 caps)
Position	Second row – No5
Lions caps	17

Relentlessly tough, with a keen intelligence and understanding of those around him, McBride was an inspirational figure as both a player and a captain.

Given the esteem in which he is held, an iconic figure seen to embody all that the touring team represents, it is amazing to recall that Willie John McBride had to play 10 Test matches for the British & Irish Lions before he actually played in a winning side. The vast majority of players who get to wear the Lions shirt never get to play as many as 10 Tests; only eight have done so in the Lions' long history. But McBride, the towering Ireland lock, was chosen for a remarkable five tours, starting in South Africa in 1962 and finishing in the same country in 1974, over the course of which he played 17 Tests. Nobody has played more and the next in the list is Dickie Jeeps, with 13 from 1955 to 1962, while Mike Gibson, Graham Price and Alun Wyn Jones have each played 12.

Those 17 Test appearances for McBride can be split into two distinct parts: on his first three tours, from 1962 to 1968, on which he played nine Tests, the Lions lost eight, drew one and won none; on the next two trips, in 1971 and 1974, he played eight Tests, the Lions lost one, drew two and won five. After the first nine Tests, and a second unsuccessful tour to South Africa in 1968, McBride did not fancy going through it all again three years later in New Zealand, where he had toured in 1966 and been thrashed. 'You reach

McBride at the centre of the action as ever as Ireland take on England in the 1970 Five Nations at Twickenham

a stage in life where you get sick of losing,' he said, and he made public his desire not to tour in 1971.

Before the squad was chosen for that 1971 tour, Carwyn James, the Lions' cerebral coach, flew over to Belfast to visit McBride and to ask him for recommendations on which players should make the tour party. Over lunch, McBride gave James his considered suggestions. The coach then said that he had heard McBride would be unavailable, to which he responded that he had been on three Lions tours and needed a rest. 'Then Carwyn sat back, took a puff on his cigarette and looked me in the eye,' McBride recalled. '"But Willie John," he said, "I need you." It knocked me off the chair, because nobody had ever said that to me before. I left that lunch and I was going to New Zealand. "This will be different," Carwyn said. "We are going to win".'

In the context of Lions history, that lunch would prove to be a seminal moment. On those first three tours, McBride had grown increasingly frustrated with the attitude that prevailed, from the Lions management in particular. Squad selection from the four nations was highly political and once on tour he felt that too many players were unable to cope with the physical onslaught that awaited from the All Blacks and Springboks and the mental challenges posed by touring countries where referees, in the time before neutral officials were introduced, often offered limited protection. For his part, as the Lions coach, James felt that McBride's vast experience and accumulated frustration could be used to good effect in New Zealand, that lessons from those earlier tours could be learned.

It cannot be said that, without him, the Lions would have gone on to lose that 1971 series to the All Blacks. But McBride was to play a hugely influential role as the Lions beat New Zealand in a series for the first time, the only time to date. He was then chosen three years later as captain for the tour to South Africa, where the Lions were sensational, going through the tour unbeaten, taming some brutal aggression from the Springboks and returning home as the Invincibles. After the tour, he was paid the ultimate compliment by Hannes Marais, his opposite number as Springboks captain in that 1974 series. 'Willie John was quite different, confidence just flowed out of him,' Marais said. 'The fact

that he could inspire guys, that he could convince them to do things they don't normally do, that was his strong point. He was a real leader of men. I'm just sorry that he wasn't on our side.' McBride is the ultimate Lions leader and the natural captain of our team of Immortals.

Much as McBride had needed some purposeful prodding from James to be convinced to travel to New Zealand, so he had needed some persuading in his younger years to take to the rugby field in the first place. At Ballymena Academy, a few miles north of his home in Moneyglass, County Antrim, he was 17 by the time he was asked by one of the teachers to play for the school. They were short of players for a game and, as one of the biggest boys at the school, they asked him to make up the numbers. By his own admission, he had little clue what he was doing in his first few games, but found that he enjoyed the physical challenge.

The fourth of five children born into a farming family, McBride's father died when he was four, which would mean that, along with his siblings, he would grow up labouring on the farm as well as going to school. Although he was a late starter on the rugby pitch, he felt that long hours spent in the potato and corn fields had inadvertently prepared him for life toiling in the second row of the scrum. 'My farm upbringing was hugely important from a physical but also a mental point of view,' he said. 'Farming in those days was very labour intensive, we didn't even have tractors then, we had to do it all ourselves. If you went out to pick a field of potatoes, it wasn't as if you could stop at half-time. You developed this thing, that you don't give in. You didn't stop when a job was half done.'

Once he had got the hang of rugby at school, his 6ft 4in frame leading him naturally into the forward pack, he played a few games for his local club at Randalstown and then moved to join Ballymena, the strongest club in the area. Among the leading players in the first team at Ballymena was Syd Millar, an astute prop who would go on to win 39 caps for Ireland and would become a significant friend and ally in McBride's career. 'He was very inexperienced when he came, he played a couple of games at No8, then we put him in the second row,' Millar said. 'He had a farmer's son's build. He was big and bony and raw, and he had that strength. But Willie learned very quickly.'

Just how quickly he learned, and how smartly he was educated at Ballymena, was clear from the fact that, having taken up the game aged 17, he was picked to make his debut for Ireland a few months before he turned 22. He was not just a big man, he was athletic with it, and was a natural ballplayer with hands the size of dustbin lids. At the time, he had never even been to an international match, so it was a shock to the system to be travelling to London and playing in the Five Nations in front of packed stands at Twickenham. Millar was alongside him in the pack, but this was a young and callow Ireland team, and England ran out comfortable 16–0 winners. In fact, Ireland lost all three games played in the tournament that season – the fourth, a draw against Wales, was postponed and played early the next season – and in terms of results McBride endured a difficult start to his international career. He would have to wait for his eighth game for Ireland before a match was won.

Yet he had done enough in those first three international appearances to catch the eye of the Lions selectors and, when the 30-man squad for the 1962 tour to South Africa was named, he was

The 1971 Lions squad to tour New Zealand: (back, left to right) Doug Smith (manager), Mike Gibson, Chris Rea, Ian McLauchlan, Fergus Slattery, Sandy Carmichael, Derek Quinnell, Mike Roberts, John Spencer, Sean Lynch, Delme Thomas, Mick Hipwell, Peter Dixon, Carwyn James (coach); (middle) Arthur Lewis, Willie John McBride, Mervyn Davies, Gordon Brown, John Dawes, Bob Hiller, John Bevan, Alistair Biggar, John Taylor; (front) Ray McLoughlin, Ray Hopkins, John Pullin, Gareth Edwards, Barry John, Frank Laidlaw, Gerald Davies, JPR Williams, David Duckham

one of eight Ireland players, despite their poor run of results. Still only 21 at the start of the tour, McBride did not know what to expect in South Africa, but he played his way into the Test team for the final two Tests, the first two having been miserably low-scoring affairs, a 3–3 draw in Johannesburg followed by a 3–0 defeat in Durban. The third Test was another close contest, but the Lions were thumped 34–14 in the final Test in Bloemfontein.

They had fallen short and McBride's mind had been opened to the sort of physical challenge posed in the southern hemisphere, which was different to anything faced in the Five Nations. 'It was the national game in South Africa and we went there and we had nice people,' he said. 'We had a nice manager, who was ex-Navy, and we had a nice captain, Arthur Smith. A nice man, a quiet man. Nice men don't survive in South Africa. Or New Zealand, for that matter.'

The next two tours with the Lions were not much better. There were more curious selections from the amateur 'blazers' for the tour to New Zealand in 1966, including a lack of a specialist openside and the controversial choice of Mike Campbell-Lamerton, the Scotland lock, as captain. The frustrations of the tour included local referees celebrating when the Lions' opponents scored and acts of violence regularly going unpunished. The Lions were hammered 4–0 in the Test series. 'It was total nonsense,' McBride said. 'The two guys in the running for the captaincy were Ray McLoughlin and Alun Pask, but the committee said, "We'll pick Campbell-Lamerton, he's a leader in the British Army". Campbell-Lamerton was a devout Catholic, he came from church and said he had lit a candle for the Lions. I said, "Mike, there's only one thing that works with these bastards and that's going out on the field and kicking the shit out of them".'

There was more woeful officiating on the tour to South Africa two years later, including a sending off against Eastern Transvaal for John O'Shea, the Wales prop, when he threw a punch in response to punches being aimed at him. While he was walking back to the changing rooms along the touchline, O'Shea was pelted with oranges and beer cans from local spectators. As he reached

the tunnel, a spectator ran out of the crowd and punched O'Shea. A melee ensued and McBride, seeking to protect O'Shea, waded in to punch the spectator and was escorted away by police. In the Test series, the Lions scraped a draw in the second Test in Port Elizabeth, but lost the other three Tests on a trip where the tour socialising got out of hand at times. 'We weren't good enough,' McBride said. 'As forwards, we were inferior to the hard-grafting South African packs that dominated possession and played a tough, physical game. Physically we could prepare, but mentally we were not strong enough.'

Once McBride had been talked around by Carwyn James for the 1971 tour to New Zealand, there was a fierce determination that lessons would be heeded from those disappointing tours of the 1960s. It was not simply a question of the Lions needing to ready themselves for greater physical challenges and committing to match the aggression they would meet, but taking on their opponents with a new self-belief. This approach was underscored by the development of that group of players from the 1968 tour – the likes of Gareth Edwards, Barry John,

Gerald Davies, John Taylor, Mike Gibson and McBride – and the way they had performed in international rugby since, with the Welsh team in particular growing into a formidable force, with a group of gifted backs. 'For the first time, we were on the right lines,' McBride said. 'We said, "We're going to run at them". It was a whole new philosophy.'

The Lions were getting serious. But they were also mindful of the intensity that would be brought by the All Blacks and even the provincial sides before the Test series, keen to put the tourists off their stride, with potentially scant protection from home referees. In the tour match against Canterbury in Christchurch before the first

McBride tussles for lineout ball during Ireland's Five Nations victory over England at Twickenham in 1972

Test, they realised what they were up against when Sandy Carmichael, the prop, was punched in the face so many times that he was ruled out of the tour and Fergus Slattery was concussed by a punch that left him needing dental reconstruction.

These Lions, though, were made of stern stuff. They won that match against Canterbury and sent a message to the All Blacks that they would not be intimidated. John Dawes, the Welsh centre, was a respected captain, and McBride rallied the forwards. The first Test in Dunedin was a ferocious contest and the All Blacks threw everything they had at the Lions, but Ian McLauchlan scored his chargedown try and the Lions tackled and kept on tackling, preventing the home side from scoring a try. When they scraped across the line for a 9–3 victory, McBride had finally got that first Test victory in a Lions shirt, nine years after his first attempt. 'Something changed in Willie John after that first Test victory,' Mervyn Davies said. 'By all accounts, on previous tours, he had enjoyed the social side of touring and was known to be a bit rowdy. But winning in New Zealand opened his eyes: he saw what feats the Lions were capable of and it inspired his play.

McBride used his experience of previous Lions tours to become a key figure on the 1971 tour to New Zealand and then lead the 1974 tour to South Africa

He discovered that Lions rugby did not have to be a hopeless cause.'

Indeed, the Lions' backs kept running at New Zealand, the forwards kept standing up to the onslaughts aimed at them, and they succeeded in playing some wonderful rugby, winning the third Test to take a 2–1 series lead into the final match in Auckland. In a desperately tight contest, the Lions scored a crucial try from Peter Dixon, the flanker, with McBride helping him over the line from short range, before JPR Williams' drop-goal ensured they would draw the match and win the series. Their togetherness, skill and toughness had enabled them to become the first Lions team to win a series in New Zealand, sweeter still for those who had endured the frustrations of previous tours. Carwyn James had been right, it was different this time, and McBride would not be declaring himself unavailable next time. 'After three losses, that was really special,' he said. 'It set the standards for what was to come later on.'

That was a tour on which McBride's leadership qualities came very much to the fore and in 1973 he was made captain of Ireland. A year later, he led the side to their first Five Nations title since 1951, a far cry from those early internationals when he had to wait so long for a win in a green shirt. After a narrow defeat to France and a creditable draw against that powerful Welsh team, Ireland claimed a thrilling victory over England, scoring four tries to one in a 26–21 win. McBride was his usual self at the heart of the pack and also demonstrated the quality of his handling in the build-up to a try for John Moloney, scooping up the loose ball on Ireland's 10-metre line, swiftly transferring out to Arthur McMaster, whose kick ahead was fumbled by Alan Old, presenting the chance for Moloney to score. A victory over Scotland then clinched the title for McBride's side.

The Ireland captaincy, though, came with its own unique challenges, with the Troubles raging across his native Northern Ireland. An all-Ireland team was not to everybody's taste, others objected to a Protestant captaining a team of mainly Catholics, and death threats were directed at McBride, who, working in a bank in Belfast, saw some of the worst moments of the Troubles. Security was required at the family home and outside his room at the team hotel. 'I wasn't going to run away from my responsibilities, so I stuck with it,' he said. 'But those were difficult years.'

With his extensive knowledge of previous Lions tours and the reputation he had developed, McBride was a natural choice, aged 34, to lead the tour to South Africa in 1974. Over the course of that summer, in such an unforgiving climate his leadership of a brilliant team would see him become known as one of the great captains in the history of British and Irish sport. He knew exactly what would be required in South Africa and laid out the task ahead to his squad

McBride leads his team off the flight back from South Africa at Heathrow following their unbeaten 1974 tour

in the starkest terms before they departed. 'I've been to South Africa before, there's going to be a lot of physical intimidation, a lot of cheating,' he said. 'So if you're not up for a fight, there's the door.' No one left, the message had landed, the Lions would stick together, with a harmony between those selected for the Test team and those who would play the midweek matches, and they were determined that a backward step would not be taken.

On the hard grounds, the Lions would also play some scintillating rugby. They won the first Test 12–3 in heavy conditions in Cape Town, then scored five tries to none in an exhilarating performance to win the second Test 28–9 in Pretoria, a record defeat for the Springboks. JJ Williams scored two tries and McBride played a vital part in the second of those, a reminder of his skill with ball in hand, all too often overlooked. After Phil Bennett had burst out of his own 22, McBride was on hand when the fly half was tackled, handing quickly on to Mervyn Davies. McBride then took a quick return ball from Davies, drawing his man and delivering a lovely pass in one motion to Gordon Brown, who sent Gareth Edwards on his way before Williams, in the right-hand corner, completed one of the Lions' great scores.

The third Test in Port Elizabeth would see the Springboks live up to the worst aspects of their reputation. They had been humiliated in Pretoria and were intent on exacting revenge, with violence if necessary, and the Test was scarred by mass punch-ups between the teams. Warned as they had been by McBride, the Lions knew what was coming, and they were prepared. They had formulated a response that, if they sensed that trouble was brewing, they would each aim a punch at the nearest Springbok. It became known as the famed '99' call. 'There were a few incidents on that tour where the opposition didn't like the way we were dominating,' McBride said. 'I said if any of this happens, we will have this call, it was originally 999, but that was too slow. If this happens, we all just lash into them. They won't know what to do and the referee won't know what to do.'

It was not a pretty sight, but it was undoubtedly effective. The Lions had conclusively withstood South Africa's attempts to intimidate them and had outplayed them, too, with Williams scoring two more tries in a 26–9 victory. The series was won

'It was on African soil that the big man from Ballymena cemented his status as, arguably, the greatest Lion of them all.' – *Mervyn Davies*

and McBride was carried aloft on the shoulders of his teammates from the field. Before the celebrations began, though, he insisted that all the Test team walk over to the rest of the Lions squad, sitting in the stands, and applaud them for their part in the success of the tour. True leadership in action.

The final Test in Johannesburg was drawn and the Lions had gone through the whole tour unbeaten, an astonishing achievement, and a measure of how far they had come from McBride's early tours. 'It was on African soil,' Mervyn Davies said, 'that the big man from Ballymena cemented his status as, arguably, the greatest Lion of them all.'

Richard Hill, a hugely influential presence on the Lions tours to South Africa in 1997 and Australia four years later

RICHARD HILL

Name	Richard Hill
Birthdate	23 May 1973
Birthplace	Dormansland
Country	England (71 caps)
Position	Blindside flanker – No6
Lions caps	5

A flanker that other players, both backs and forwards, simply loved to have in their team. He did the jobs that others might not have fancied and much more besides.

One of the great beauties of rugby union is the sheer variety of roles required to make up a team. The most obvious appeal of this necessary diversity is that the sport, at every level, can accept players who come in a range of shapes and sizes, from the prop forward to the winger and everything in between. But there is also a place in a rugby team for the extrovert and the introvert, for the skilful ball handler and the tough tackler, from the playmakers who enjoy kicking, passing and running with the ball to those who prefer the less glamorous roles, grafting away from the limelight, relishing the close-quarters physical contact,

hitting rucks and frustrating the opposition, players who may not touch the ball more than a handful of times in a match, yet still get through a mountain of meaningful work, the unseen stuff that helps to knit the rest of the team together.

Few players typify such a player better than Richard Hill, the flanker whose natural power and intuitive reading of the game made him a remarkably consistent performer for Saracens, England and the British & Irish Lions. Temperamentally and technically, Hill was perfectly suited to playing blindside flanker, although his skillset was so broad that he was capable of packing down in any of the three back-row positions

Hill celebrates the Lions' series-clinching victory over South Africa in Durban in 1997

and played plenty of big games on the openside. The work of a No7 tends to be far more conspicuous than the efforts of a No6 and Hill's insatiable work rate in carrying out those unseen tasks was often overlooked. 'You might have had to play alongside him or to coach him to realise just how good he was,' Ian McGeechan, his coach for the Lions, said. 'But once you had, you were certainly in no doubt.'

Over the course of an international career that ran from 1997 to 2005, Hill was never dropped by England, only missing games when the inevitable injuries intervened. His low-profile role

meant that he was one of the less famous members of England's World Cup-winning side in 2003 – which suited him nicely – but every teammate recognised him as one of the players most crucial to that success, still the only World Cup victory for a northern hemisphere nation in 10 attempts. 'Without question, the best rugby player England have ever had,' was the view of Matt Dawson, the England scrum half, although Hill himself would scoff at any such hyperbole.

He was a hugely influential presence on two Lions tours, helping them to a series victory in South Africa in 1997, and four years later tearing into Australia, who lost the first Test and were trailing in the second when Hill was concussed by a horribly violent challenge. He missed the second half and, such was his importance to the Lions' efforts, it was felt by many to be the pivotal moment of the whole tour: the Wallabies rallied to win the second Test and, with Hill absent from the decider, eventually ran out as narrow series winners. It was not just teammates who understood the full extent of Hill's value to a side, it was his opponents too. Serge Betsen, a fellow flanker, who knew a thing or two about attending to the unseen duties on a rugby field, perhaps summed up Hill's role best, having faced him a number of times for France. 'He works in the shadows, in the darkness,' Betsen said. 'And in this place Richard Hill is very, very important.'

He may have felt a natural aversion to the spotlight, but Hill has always had a fondness for playing under floodlights, dating back to his childhood growing up in Salisbury. The family home was little more than a drop-kick away from the local rugby club and, whenever Salisbury were playing a midweek match, Hill would notice the glare of the lights and beg his parents to

be taken along. Once at the game, his parents, John and Penny, would sit and watch, while he played with a ball on an adjacent pitch with his friends, always keeping half an eye on proceedings in the big match and absorbing what he saw.

His father had played rugby and hockey, helping to set up the junior section at Salisbury and Hill followed his brother, Tim, who was six years older, into the ranks, and he loved the game from an early age. 'I don't remember standing out as a youngster,' he said. 'Apparently, the coaches said that I had something special about me, that I could read the game. I just remember being a roly-poly kid who wanted to run with the ball.' When he was playing with his friends, he would pretend to be Dean Richards or Peter Winterbottom, England's two most prominent back-rowers of the time. Not for Hill the childhood reverie of wanting to grow up as a goal-kicking fly half, or one of the other flashy backs. He knew where he was heading.

His rugby education stepped up another level at his secondary school, Bishop Wordsworth's, a state grammar school in Salisbury with a strong rugby tradition. It just so happened that his namesake, another Richard Hill, who went on to play scrum half for Bath and England, had attended the same school a few years earlier. After school, he went on to study sports studies and geography at the West London Institute of Higher Education, a college with close links to Saracens. The time was right for him to move on from Salisbury and he would stay with Saracens for the rest of his career. He also made it into the England Under 21 team and on the night before his debut, he found himself rooming with a fellow back-rower called Lawrence Dallaglio, someone he would spend a considerable amount of time with in the years to come.

Hill was 23 by the time he was given his England debut, against Scotland at Twickenham in the 1997 Five Nations, and Dallaglio was alongside him in the back row. At the time, Jack Rowell, the England coach, was intent on playing flankers with plenty of bulk, so Dallaglio was at blindside and Hill, at 6ft 2in and 17 stone, found his place on the openside, with Tim Rodber at No8. Rowell's policy came at the expense of a more traditional openside flanker, in particular Neil Back, who had to bide his time until a new England coach before he would establish himself in the side.

It did not take long for Hill to settle and he played all four Five Nations matches in 1997. In a team that was scoring plenty of points, his work rate and his knack for appearing on the scene whenever a teammate needed support were quickly noticed, and on his debut at Murrayfield he succeeded in the job he had been given, to prevent Gregor Townsend, the gifted Scotland fly half, from showing his talents. 'I'm particularly pleased with Richard Hill,' Rowell said. 'You just don't play against a more dangerous opponent than Townsend, who is world class, but the new boy didn't miss a trick.'

Beyond snuffing out opposing attacks, Hill even managed to chip in with two tries of his own in his first four international appearances. In his second game in Dublin, England ran riot against Ireland and Hill crossed for one of six tries in a 46–6 victory. As an England attack drifted left, Austin Healey picked up from a ruck 20 metres out, dummied a pass to Phil de Glanville and then, as he was caught, looked up to see Hill timing his run beautifully late to take a scoring pass.

Hill and his great friend Jonny Wilkinson (left), on the 2001 Lions tour to Australia

Against Wales in Cardiff two matches later, England were again in dominant form, scoring another four tries. For the third of them, Jeremy Guscott ran onto a pass from De Glanville 25 metres from the tryline and set off on a mesmerising, jinking run into the Wales 22. The Welsh defence certainly didn't know where he was going. Almost certainly, Guscott didn't know where he was going. But Hill did, arriving just as Guscott had sucked in three red-shirted defenders, taking the offload and scoring under the posts, as England won 34–13. Those junior coaches at Salisbury, who had reckoned Hill was a decent reader of the game, they might just have been onto something.

Only a defeat against France at Twickenham prevented England from clinching the grand slam during that Five Nations, Rowell's last tournament in charge before Clive Woodward took over as coach. They had scored 15 tries in their four matches and, when the British & Irish Lions team to travel to South Africa that summer was named by McGeechan, England had a record 18 representatives in a squad of 35. Despite his recent introduction to the international scene, Hill was among them, along with Dallaglio, Rodber and Back. The Springboks had won the World Cup two years earlier, having recently emerged from sporting isolation with the fall of the apartheid regime. It was the

Lions' first visit to South Africa for 17 years and the Springboks were sure to provide highly motivated opposition. The home side were firm favourites.

This was also the first Lions tour of the professional era, with the move away from amateurism made following the 1995 World Cup. As a result, the Lions squad included a number of players who had moved

Hill takes to the field before the Lions' victory in the first Test of the 2001 series in Brisbane, where he was in outstanding form

back to union from rugby league, the likes of Scott Gibbs, John Bentley, Alan Tait and Scott Quinnell. Rugby league was a long way ahead of the 15-man code in terms of the value it placed on defence and the former league contingent brought with them a commitment to defending that the rest of the squad would take on board.

Defence would become a huge focus for the Lions back row and, after their success playing together in the Five Nations, McGeechan liked the look of the England back-row combination of Dallaglio, Hill and Rodber, once Eric Miller, the Ireland No8, had been ruled out with illness. So Hill, once again, found himself on the openside and facing a back row of bone-jarring physicality in the first Test in Cape Town. This would be a step up from anything he had previously faced. 'Their back row were totally uncompromising,' he said. 'Particularly André Venter and Ruben Kruger, unbelievably physical, but in a largely legitimate way. I'd only played in four Five Nations matches by that stage and the physicality of the tackle wasn't anywhere close. I'd never imagined anything like it before.'

He was given an early taste when Gary Teichmann, the No8, came charging off the back of the scrum. But Hill was up to the challenge, meeting the Springbok captain head on, and, with help from Rodber, stopping him in his tracks. Gibbs followed up by thumping into Andre Snyman and dumping him into the turf. This was the sort of defence that was going to be needed. South Africa led 9–8 at half-time and 16–15 going into the last 10 minutes, but the Lions were finishing the stronger, and late tries from Matt Dawson and Alan Tait earned them a 26–15 victory, to the delight of the thronged Lions fans in the stands.

The Lions' all-English back row had been outstanding and they were retained, en bloc, for the second Test in Durban. The Springboks had not been expecting defeat and had been savaged by the local media. 'You could feel the genuine rage in them that we'd beaten them in the first Test,' Hill said. The game in Durban was later described by Dallaglio as the most physically intense of his entire career. Hill and Dallaglio were both 24, but they were up to the task. Although South Africa were on top for large parts of the game, their goal-kicking was woeful, Neil Jenkins' boot kept the Lions in touch and then Jeremy

'By nature, I am a foot soldier. You need foot soldiers, and that's what I do best.'
– Richard Hill

Guscott sealed another victory with a late drop-goal. Against the odds, the Lions had won the series and Hill had played a leading role at the end of his first season in international rugby. 'He was so competitive, such a good reader of the game, he always seemed to be near the ball,' McGeechan said. 'He was just incredible in that series.'

The next season, Woodward had taken the reins with England and one of his first tasks was a daunting meeting with New Zealand at Old Trafford. Dallaglio was now captain and the back row to face the All Blacks saw him starting at No6 with Hill at No7 and Tony Diprose at No8, with Rodber injured. The first half did not go according to plan and, with England trailing 15–3, Woodward replaced Diprose with Neil Back at the break. Back came on at openside, Dallaglio moved to No8 and Hill onto the blindside. All three were in their natural positions.

England were unable to claw their way back in that game, but Woodward had seen something in that back-row combination. Dallaglio had the power and pace carrying from the base, Back was a natural poacher at the ruck and Hill's industry, breakdown work and support play provided the rest. A couple of weeks after that defeat at Old Trafford, they started together against the All Blacks at Twickenham and England secured a thrilling 26–26 draw, with Hill on hand to score as Will Greenwood was brought down just short, and making a stunning try-saving tackle on Jeff Wilson. 'I think the strength we had was that we understood each other's strengths and we played to those strengths,' Back said.

They started to spend a lot of time together off the field and would go on to be England's most capped back-row combination together, with 39 starts as a unit. As their reputation grew, they became known as the Holy Trinity. England were knocked out of the 1999 World Cup at the quarter-final stage, but Woodward remained at the helm and the team would grow stronger together over the next four years, by which time the back-row triumvirate would know each other's games inside out.

All three were selected in the British & Irish Lions squad to tour Australia in 2001 under Graham Henry, a New Zealander, who was the first from outside the home nations to coach the Lions. Dallaglio, however, was ruled out early through a knee problem and Back missed the first Test through injury. Starting at the Gabba in Brisbane alongside Martin Corry and Scott Quinnell, Hill was sensational as the Lions won the first Test 29–13. And Back was fit to return for the second Test in Melbourne, taking his place at No7

Nathan Grey, the Australia centre, leads with his elbow and hits Hill in the head, a controversial and pivotal moment in the 2001 Lions series

Hill was a major player in England's rise to become World Cup winners in 2003, still the only northern hemisphere team to lift the Webb Ellis Cup

with Hill in his natural blindside role and Quinnell at No8, an even more potent back row.

In the first half, Hill kept up his standards from the first Test and the Lions were well on top, leading 11–3 in the 32nd minute, when Keith Wood made a brilliant break, supported by Martin Johnson, who passed on to Hill. Seeing the pass going towards Hill, Nathan Grey, the Australia centre, launched himself, elbow first, at Hill's head, knocking him to the ground. Hill attempted to continue, but was unable to return after half-time. Astonishingly, Grey's assault went unpunished, to the fury of the Lions management, who felt that their outstanding player had been deliberately targeted. Australia went on to win that game and clinched the series in Sydney.

'The loss of Richard was a huge blow for us,' Henry said. 'He is one of the top flankers in the world, if not the best. I firmly believe that his injury was a major factor in Australia winning the series. When you are robbed of a player who has his wide range of skills it is bound to have an effect.'

A chance to exact a measure of revenge on the Wallabies would come in the white shirt of England, at the World Cup in Australia two years later. By then, England had built themselves into the number one ranked side in the world, they had beaten the All Blacks in New Zealand, and they were favourites to win the World Cup. But in their first pool game, against Georgia in Perth, Hill injured his hamstring and there seemed a chance that he would not play in the tournament again. For all their strength, England were rarely at their best in the pool stages and struggled in the first half of the quarter-final against Wales, before eventually pulling through.

Woodward had not sent Hill home because he knew of his importance to the team, should he regain fitness. By the time of the semi-final against France, Hill's hamstring was serviceable again and, although he had not played a match for more than a month, he was straight back into the starting line-up. The Holy Trinity were back together, England produced their most complete performance of the tournament to beat France, and went on to win the World Cup against the Wallabies.

There was not a weak link in that England team, from the dazzling brilliance of Jason Robinson at full back to a solid front row of Trevor Woodman, Steve Thompson and Phil Vickery. But the back row, who had been through so many battles together, were at the heart of the success. 'When has there ever been a better England back row than Richard Hill, Neil Back and Lawrence Dallaglio?' Vickery said. 'Still to this day there hasn't.'

When Martin Johnson stepped down as England captain after the World Cup, Hill's name was mentioned as a potential successor. But such exposed positions were not for him, he felt he was happier doing his work in the shadows. 'By nature, I am a foot soldier,' Hill said. 'You need foot soldiers, and that's what I do best.'

Seán O'Brien, the versatile flanker who could be relied on to produce influential performances when the stakes were at their highest

SEÁN O'BRIEN

Name	Seán O'Brien
Birthdate	14 February 1987
Birthplace	Carlow
Country	Ireland (56 caps)
Position	Openside flanker – No7
Lions caps	5

He might not crop up in lists of the game's greatest openside flankers, because O'Brien could play in any back-row position, but he was brilliant wearing No7 for the Lions.

Apart from being the best player in their position from England, Ireland, Scotland and Wales, any player who has excelled for the British & Irish Lions has also managed to get their timing right. Those who have shone in the famous red shirt have been fortunate enough, first and foremost, to be fit at the crucial stage of the four-year cycle, then to have the skill and temperament to play to the best of their ability in such a pressurised environment. Whenever he took the field for the Lions, in two Tests on the 2013 tour to Australia and all three in New Zealand four years later, he seemed to be near the peak of his formidable powers.

A rumbustious, multi-faceted flanker, equally comfortable at No6 or No7, he suffered more than his fair share of injuries during a 10-year international career and a player of his ability might have been expected to win more than his tally of 56 Ireland caps. But whenever a big game came around, O'Brien could be relied on to perform, whether that was for Leinster in Heineken Cup finals, for Ireland winning Six Nations titles or during those two Test series for the Lions.

With ball in hand, O'Brien was like a rubber ball, bouncing defenders

O'Brien in action against a Combined Country XV on the 2013 Lions tour, when he played his way into the Test team midway through the series and quickly made an impact

from his path, but also blessed with the acceleration to go around them when he chose. He was ferocious in defence and, despite standing 6ft 2in, with a low centre of gravity that made him incredibly difficult to shift at the breakdown. In the first Test of the 2017 series against the All Blacks, his support play meant that he was on hand to score one of the greatest Lions tries. In the second Test, he gave one of the finest all-round performances to ensure that the Lions stayed in the series.

Always a fiendishly competitive opponent, O'Brien was undoubtedly one of those players capable of finding another level to his game when big prizes were at stake. 'The impact he had on big games was extraordinary,' Rob Kearney, his former Ireland and Lions teammate, said. 'At his best, he was close to unplayable.'

Like Tadhg Furlong, who also starred in that Lions tour to New Zealand, O'Brien came from a farming family and enjoyed a strong background in junior club rugby, rather than the increasingly professionalised private school system that has served Leinster so well in recent times. The O'Brien family cattle farm is in the verdant countryside outside Tullow in County Carlow, just over an hour's drive south-west of Dublin. From the Under 7s upwards, he became part of the fabric at the local club at Tullow and played Gaelic football for the Fighting Cocks. His father, Seán Snr, had played there and later became the club president, while his sister, Alex, has captained the women's team.

He has remained close to his home community, regularly coaching back at Tullow during his playing days. After he had retired from professional rugby, he would return to Tullow to work on the family farm. True to his roots, at the age of 36 he would also turn out both for Tullow at rugby, in the unfamiliar position of fly half, and also for the Fighting Cocks. Some professionals find it hard to return to lower levels once their best days are behind them; O'Brien, nicknamed the Tullow Tank, clearly relished returning to the clubs that had set him on his way.

Once it had become clear that his talent was outgrowing the local club scene, around the age of 18, he had moved to study commerce at University College Dublin and joined the Leinster academy. He furthered his reputation with his

performances for his university and was soon ready to join some stellar names in the Leinster senior squad. 'I'd heard about him at UCD,' Brian O'Driscoll, the Ireland captain at the time, said. 'He came into Leinster training and I didn't really get what the coaching staff were talking about for the first week or two. And then I played a game with him and I thought, "Ah, yes, OK . . ."' When O'Brien graduated from the academy to join the first-team squad, his first pay cheque from Leinster was spent on a downpayment for a new tractor for the family farm.

The wheels of his professional career were in motion and he had become part of the Leinster squad at an auspicious time. After years in the shadow of Munster, the Dublin-based team were about to embark on a remarkable run of success, first under the coaching of Michael Cheika, then his celebrated successor, Joe Schmidt. The Irish professional system was beginning to make the most of the country's limited playing pool, taking the best of Munster and Leinster, their two leading provinces, with different cultures and strengths, and blending them together in the national team. Munster had traditionally provided the forward

With ball in hand, O'Brien was like a rubber ball, bouncing defenders from his path.

power, Leinster the skilful back play. But Leinster were catching up fast, with a potent pack of their own.

At the end of his first full season with the senior squad, O'Brien would be a replacement in the 2009 Heineken Cup final alongside a host of players who would become household names in Ireland: Brian O'Driscoll, Johnny Sexton, Gordon D'Arcy, Cian Healy, Jamie Heaslip. Leinster won their first Heineken Cup, beating Leicester Tigers in the final, and a number of their players had featured in the Six Nations, where Ireland had completed their first grand slam since 1948. A new age was dawning in Irish rugby.

It was not long before O'Brien joined them in the Ireland team, making his debut from the bench against Fiji in the November international against Fiji. He nailed down a place in the starting line-up during the 2011 Six Nations, with a rare outing at No8 against Italy before switching to blindside flanker for the next four games. He was man of the match against the Italians and throughout the tournament

demonstrated that his ball-carrying could bring a different dimension to Ireland's forward effort. During the narrow defeat to Wales in Cardiff, he set off on one astonishing carry, hitting the ball at pace on the Wales 22, swerving immediately to pick out a hole in the defensive line, then stepping nimbly off his left foot. Three metres from the line, it took four Welsh defenders to bring him down. Few back-row players combine power and footwork to such effect.

That Six Nations was a tournament of mixed fortunes for Ireland, but O'Brien had announced himself on the international stage, finishing as one of the nominees for player of the tournament, his place in the Ireland back row cemented. He was just as impressive for Leinster, who won their second Heineken Cup in three seasons with a breathless second-half comeback to overhaul Northampton Saints in the final. They had been 22–6 down at half-time, but then scored 27 unanswered points to crown Schmidt's first season with the major trophy in European club rugby.

Bigger prizes still were on offer at the World Cup in New Zealand later that year, where hopes were high for Ireland that they could progress beyond the quarter-finals for the

O'Brien stretches over to score for the Lions against Melbourne Rebels on the tour to Australia in 2013

first time, and O'Brien was in regal form in the pool stages. Against Russia in Rotorua, he demonstrated the fearsome power of his ball-carrying, running onto a pass from Isaac Boss and swatting aside a string of defenders to score his second international try. In the biggest game of the pool stage, Ireland took on Australia in Auckland, and O'Brien was shifted to openside flanker, where he enjoyed an outstanding game, his ball-carrying a constant thorn in the Wallabies' side, while a late try-saving tackle on Will Genia helped Ireland to squeeze out a 15–6 victory.

As a result, they finished top of their pool, avoiding South Africa in the quarter-finals, and facing Wales in Wellington instead. Alas, Wales were a gathering force under Warren Gatland and Ireland fell at the quarter-final hurdle once more, but O'Brien finished as one of five players of the tournament, despite his side missing out on the last four. It had been quite some year and his renown had now extended to the global stage.

Gatland was to be head coach of the Lions for the first time in 2013 and, after Wales had just won consecutive Six Nations titles, the 37-man squad to tour Australia included 15 Wales players, 10 from England, nine from Ireland and three from Scotland. O'Brien was included along with Jamie Heaslip, his back-row colleague as a No8 with Leinster and Ireland, but they knew that there would be stiff competition for Test places with the Welsh loose forwards, who had been so impressive in the Six Nations, Dan Lydiate, Justin Tipuric, Taulupe Faletau and Sam Warburton, who was named as Lions captain.

For the first Test in Brisbane, Heaslip started, but O'Brien missed out. The Lions won 23–21 in a desperately tense game, but O'Brien came onto the bench for the second Test in Melbourne, determined to make his mark. He was given 18 minutes as a replacement in that second Test, coming on as the Lions were attempting to repel a swelling wave

O'Brien escapes the clutches of Codie Taylor during the second Test against the All Blacks in 2017, when he gave a fine all-round display of his talents

of Australian attacks, and he made his presence felt immediately. In his short time on the pitch, he carried with purpose, tackled hard and, although the Lions slipped to an agonising 16–15 defeat, O'Brien had made a strong case for inclusion for what would be a momentous series decider in Sydney.

Warburton was injured, so O'Brien played at openside flanker, with Lydiate on the blindside and Faletau at No8. The pace of the game was frenetic and O'Brien once again made an instant impact. After Genia had dropped the kick-off, the Lions were immediately on the attack and O'Brien made a powerful short, straight burst from 15 metres out, dragging both George Smith and James Horwill backwards in the tackle. The Wallabies defence scrambled to recover, but Alex Corbisiero dived over from short range and the Lions were on their way. O'Brien was a hive of industry throughout, topping his side's tackle count with 13, as the Lions produced a masterful performance to complete a historic 41–16 victory. After previous disappointments in 2009, 2005 and 2001, this was the Lions' first series victory for 16 years, and O'Brien had produced the goods on the big occasion once again.

Back with Ireland, Schmidt's success with Leinster had seen him promoted to become Ireland head coach and his knack for winning trophies would continue. Schmidt's third game in charge of the national team almost resulted in a victory over New Zealand in Dublin, with Ireland denied only by Ryan Crotty's late try. For O'Brien, though, the attritional nature of the position he played began to take its toll with an unfortunate sequence of injuries. In that defeat to the All Blacks, he sustained the shoulder injury that would mean he missed Ireland's title triumph in the 2014 Six Nations. Further setbacks with his shoulder were followed by a hamstring injury, meaning he spent more than a year out of the international game, but he came back for Ireland's second game of the 2015 Six Nations against France.

He settled back in quickly and, by the last round of matches, Ireland were in position to win a second consecutive title as they travelled to Murrayfield to face Scotland. They had not won consecutive outright titles since 1949, a significant achievement was at stake, and, if they won, they still needed plenty of points to stay ahead of England and Wales on points difference.

Lining up at openside, O'Brien scored two tries for the only time in his international career.

The first came when Devin Toner palmed down a lineout on the Scotland 22, O'Brien took possession and immediately spotted a chink in the defence. He surged through and in the blink of an eye was up against the last defender, Blair Cowan. He stepped off his right foot, swerved through the challenge and dived over to score a brilliant try. That combination of rapid acceleration and physical power, which had always been such a hallmark of his play, had clearly survived his spell away from international rugby. His second try was from nearer the line, but involved a swift dummy, quick feet in a congested area and a powerful finish, incredibly difficult to stop from close range.

'He's not a particularly tall guy, but there's this powerfulness that you don't anticipate,' O'Driscoll said. 'It's farmer-strength, that raw strength you can't generate in the gym, no matter how hard you try. He's a brilliant teammate who'll empty his tank every time.' Ireland won the title on points difference from England by six points. Another big occasion,

another bravura performance from O'Brien.

On the 2013 Lions tour to Australia, Sam Warburton and O'Brien had largely been used interchangeably. Warburton started the first Test, he came off shortly after O'Brien was introduced in the second, then O'Brien started the third when Warburton was injured. In New Zealand in 2017, Warburton was again chosen as tour captain by Gatland, but for the first Test in Auckland the Lions' coach broke with convention by leaving his captain out of the starting line-up. Warburton was named on the bench, with O'Brien getting the nod ahead of him at No7, alongside Peter O'Mahony, the blindside, and Faletau at No8.

With New Zealand leading 13–3 late in the first half, Liam Williams, the full back, took possession 10 metres from his own line, with Kieran Read, the New Zealand No8, bearing down on him. Williams stepped daringly out of trouble, evading the clutches of Aaron Cruden and Sonny Bill Williams. He was away. As he reached the halfway line, looking around for red shirts, he found Jonathan Davies to his left, who handed on to Elliot Daly on the left wing. Daly made ground and passed back inside to Davies, who was tackled just short of the line by Beauden Barrett. As he fell, Davies popped the ball up and who should he find in support, having tracked the move the length of the field, keeping up with the quickest of the

O'Brien's performance in the Lions' series-levelling victory was widely acclaimed as a masterpiece of industry, nous and power.

The Tullow Tank rumbles into action for the Lions against the Maori All Blacks in Rotorua in 2017

O'Brien started all three Tests in the Lions' 2017 series against New Zealand

backs, but Seán O'Brien. He still had to step around Aaron Smith, which he did, and then touched down to complete one of the greatest tries in Lions history. It is open to debate which is the best, but O'Brien's score will make any of the shortlists. The travelling hordes in red were in raptures, the series was alive.

Unfortunately for those spectators, that was as good as it got for the Lions in the first Test, as the All Blacks ran out comfortable 30–15 winners. Late in the Test, however, Warburton came off the bench and joined O'Brien, who played a full 80 minutes. Maro Itoje, too, came off the bench, and the Lions finished strongly, scoring a late try through Rhys Webb. Gatland liked what he had seen and, for the next two Tests, O'Brien and Warburton would start together, the Welshman on the blindside and O'Brien wearing No7.

In the second Test in Wellington, they dovetailed beautifully. O'Brien's performance in the Lions' series-levelling victory was widely acclaimed as a masterpiece of industry, nous and power, one of those games when you wonder whether there are actually two blokes wearing the red No7 shirt on the pitch. He carried strongly early in the game, attacked the breakdown hard in concert with Warburton and Itoje and defended heroically. The Lions were helped by the sending off of Sonny Bill Williams, but the All Blacks, who had not lost any of their previous 47 home matches, kept coming. And in the last minute, as Barrett chipped out of his own 22, attempting to launch one last attack, O'Brien was there to gather. He handed on to Davies and was there again with another purposeful carry a couple of phases later as the Lions wore the clock down towards victory.

For the third Test, there was a brief danger that O'Brien might be suspended, but he was cleared of swinging his arm at Waisake Naholo, to the Lions' great relief. Writing in *The Times*, Stuart Barnes, the former England fly half, said: 'O'Brien's reprieve is worth seven points for the Lions. He has become the man at the very heart of their bid to end New Zealand's iron grip on the game. He was instrumental in the series-winning third Test in Sydney in 2013. His presence is ominous to All Black eyes four years on.'

The final Test in Auckland was drawn, with O'Brien departing with a shoulder injury at the end of the first half and he was badly missed in the second half. The competitor in him remained frustrated that the Lions had not managed to secure a series win and, on his return to Ireland, he vented his frustration at some of Gatland's coaching on the tour. An indication, clearly, of the high standards he had kept throughout his career and the constant striving for success. Many would have been content with a drawn series against the world champions in their own backyard, but O'Brien wanted more.

Yet his reputation as a Lions hero, who had played key roles in two memorable series, was secure. It was no coincidence that Leinster, Ireland and the Lions all enjoyed considerable success with the Tullow Tank in their ranks, because he raised his own game, and that of players around him, in the moments that really mattered. The sign of a truly great player.

Mervyn Davies, unmistakable at 6ft 4in with his headband and shock of black hair

MERVYN DAVIES

Name	Mervyn Davies
Birthdate	9 December 1946
Birthplace	Swansea
Country	Wales (38 caps)
Position	No8
Lions caps	8

With his broad range of skills, becoming the hinge
between backs and forwards for the great Wales
and Lions teams of the 1970s, Davies reinvented
the role of a No8 for the modern game.

Some rugby players appear destined for greatness from an early age, their talent marking them apart and setting them on a separate path towards the heights of the game. Others make their own way and need a little more time to go on to fulfil their potential, perhaps needing a nudge from a coach or player, or a dose of serendipity along the way, before the realisation dawns of just how good they could be.

Although he is widely considered one of the greatest No8s to have played the game, Mervyn Davies undoubtedly falls into the latter camp. During his teenage years in Swansea, there was little to suggest that he was made of the stuff to become an international sportsman. He had played rugby for his college, to no great standard, and wondered whether basketball might actually be his sport.

There were plenty others who thought that, at 6ft 4in and less than 15 stone, he might be too gangly for the rough and tumble of serious rugby. At the age of 21, having recently moved to take up his first teaching job in Surrey, he had just joined London Welsh and had played a few games for their second and third teams. When a place in the first-team back row

Davies in typically barnstorming ball-carrying action for Wales against Scotland in the 1970 Five Nations game in Cardiff

became available due to injury early in the 1968 season, one of the club's selectors suggested the club was struggling for alternatives of sufficient calibre. 'There's a guy playing No8 for the seconds,' the selector said. 'He's not much good, but he'll guarantee you some ball at the back of the lineout.'

On that basis, Davies was given his chance in London Welsh's first team. His new teammates included Welsh internationals and he quickly realised how much he would need to improve if he were to remain in such company. But he settled swiftly, he proved a quick learner and, a few weeks later, once again due to injury to an established

player, he found himself being put forward for the national team's trial match. And he performed well enough in that trial match to earn selection to play for Wales against Scotland at Murrayfield in the opening game of the Five Nations championship. Remarkably, he was making his international debut only four months after he had been failing to impress the club selectors playing for London Welsh's second and third teams.

It was a case of being in the right place at the right time, a knack he continued to show on the field throughout his international career, as a back-row forward with an instinctive feel for the game.

Little did he realise at the time, but Davies was emerging at the same time as a group of hugely talented players of similar age, who together were about to form a national team that would go on to create a true golden era for Welsh rugby.

They would also form the nucleus for those two epic tours with the British & Irish Lions, to New Zealand in 1971 and South Africa three years later. Davies would be one of the handful of players who featured in all eight Test matches on those two tours, proving himself an immensely tough competitor with a full array of skills. Against the All Blacks, he formed a harmonious back-row combination with John Taylor, his London Welsh teammate, and Peter Dixon, of England, on the flanks. In South Africa, a similarly cohesive trio would emerge, as Roger Uttley and Fergus Slattery packed down alongside him. With his broad white headband and thick black moustache, Davies proved himself an eye-catching link between backs and forwards, forming a wonderful understanding with Gareth Edwards, the scrum half.

Up to that point, the No8 position had often been seen as a largely defensive role, but Davies always wanted to bring more to the game than that. He was still a destructive defender, but his athleticism at the base of the scrum and the tail of the lineout, along with his roaming in open play looking to link attacking moves, would change forever the role that was envisaged for a No8. 'He was only slight in stature, but he was a fine all-round player,' Edwards said. 'He ruled the roost at the lineout, he was strong in the tackle and powerful at the mauls. His delivery of lineout ball from the tail was critical to the Lions' success in 1971 and revolutionised the game.'

It may have taken him time to recognise the full extent of his talents, but, in a sense, perhaps Davies was always destined to wear the No8 shirt for Wales. At home in Swansea, he was 10 years old when he went rummaging through some drawers in his parents' bedroom and, tucked away at the bottom of one drawer, he found a neatly folded red shirt. When he pulled it out, he saw that it had the Prince of Wales feathers on the front and, when he turned it round, a white No8 on the back. He had never previously been aware of this chapter in the life of his father, Dai, who subsequently explained how he came to be in possession of the shirt.

A welder at the local power station, who had been a miner before the Second World War, Dai had played rugby for Swansea and had gone on to captain the club. After the war, the Five Nations championship did not resume until 1947, but in the previous two years a series of 'Victory Internationals' were held. They were not awarded full international status, due to the large number of absences of men still away on military duties, but Dai Davies had played for Wales in these matches, playing in the same number shirt that his son would later go on to wear 38 times.

Mervyn inherited his parents' height – his mother, Betty, was also tall at 5ft 9in – and enjoyed playing basketball, football and rugby at school. When he went on to Swansea Training College, he increasingly enjoyed the social life that came with rugby and when he went to take up his first job at a primary school in Surrey, he resolved to join the local rugby club. He was living in Guildford and joined Old Guildfordians, but soon realised that he was capable of playing a higher standard of rugby than they could offer. He knew of a club a few miles down the A3 that was a home for

exiled Welshmen and so his next staging post was Old Deer Park in Richmond, home of London Welsh.

At the time, London Welsh were one of the strongest club sides in England. The first team could boast players such as John Taylor, Geoff Evans and John Dawes, all players of international calibre, while a full back and medical student named JPR Williams had recently joined. Davies had played one game for Swansea before he left home, but that was the extent of his experience of senior club rugby, so he knew he would be playing in the club's lower teams to begin with.

He scored a hat-trick of tries in his first game for the third team, played a few matches for the seconds and then came that dubious recommendation to fill a gap in the first team, in the hope that he might use his height to supply some possession at the back of the lineout, if little else. Once he was in that first team, he found himself in a back row with Taylor, the flanker who had been on the Lions' tour to South Africa the previous summer, and Tony Gray, who had played for Wales in that year's Five Nations. Standards were high and the learning curve for Davies was steep. But he had a speed and athleticism

Davies, in action against France in 1970, overcame doubts about his size to prove that he had the physicality to thrive in international rugby

that suited the way London Welsh played, and after a few games of acclimatisation he found that he fitted in. Being able to hold his own in this company was an indication that he was getting somewhere.

On the club's Christmas tour back to Wales, the national selectors were paying close attention and Davies did enough to earn his place in the national trial game, the Probables against Possibles. The prospect of international rugby, just a few months after he had started in London Welsh's third team, seemed extraordinary, but he was about to embark on another steep learning curve. 'What startles me still is the speed with which it all happened,' he said. 'I certainly grabbed hold of the

opportunity, but I know I was in the right place at the right time.'

He was big enough and, so the Wales selectors believed, he was good enough, despite his meagre experience. This was a time when Wales' fortunes were on the turn and, when Davies played his first international match, against Scotland at Murrayfield in 1969, aged 22, he made his debut alongside JPR Williams, a teammate now for club and country. Gareth Edwards, Gerald Davies and Barry John had recently established themselves and had gone on tour with the British Lions to South Africa the previous summer. In Davies' first Five Nations championship, Wales remained unbeaten, winning three and drawing one, rounding off with a thumping 30–9 victory over England in Cardiff, which earned them the title and the triple crown.

But they were swiftly brought back down to earth, with a tour of New Zealand and Australia that featured two thumping defeats at the hands of the All Blacks. 'We went, fresh-faced and innocent, to New Zealand and Australia, and we thought we were quite good,' Davies said. 'We learned just how poor we actually were.'
Just as Davies had learned to raise his own standards quickly by being thrown in at the deep end, first with London Welsh, then the national team, so those defeats to New Zealand had made plain to Wales what would be needed collectively to become the best in the world. They were young enough to improve and they had been shown the way forward. 'Something changed for the Welsh players as we conceded two huge defeats,' Davies said. 'We returned vowing never to suffer such indignity and humiliation again.'

Davies and John Taylor, back-row colleagues for London Welsh, Wales and the Lions

In the Five Nations two years later, they completed a first Welsh grand slam for 19 years, demonstrating that hard-nosed determination by grinding out victories in tight matches in Murrayfield and Paris. That success ensured that Welsh players, under the coaching of Carwyn James, would form the bulk of the Lions squad to tour New Zealand that summer. Six of the original squad came from London Welsh, a remarkable representation for one club. Davies would later move back to Wales to rejoin Swansea, but there was no doubting his good fortune in joining London Welsh at such a time.

That hardened attitude that the Welsh players had brought back from New Zealand crystallised into a fierce desire to do themselves proud against the All Blacks, where the Lions had never won. There was a feeling that previous tours had perhaps been excessively social and it would be different this time. 'We didn't consider the Lions tour to be a bit of a jolly,' Davies said. 'We wanted to go there and win the series. We had genuine desire backed up by ruthless commitment.'

Davies made his own statement of intent in the early stages of the tour, when the Lions came up

*'He won the ball at the back of the lineout, steadied everything, always took possession forward. He was the perfect No8.'
– Ian McLauchlan*

against King Country in Wanganui, a team that included Colin Meads. Nicknamed the Pine Tree due to his stature and solidity in the second row, Meads was the standard bearer of the tough, uncompromising forward play that the New Zealanders saw as the defining characteristic of their national team. That day in Wanganui, Davies saw his opportunity to cut the Pine Tree down to size. When the ball was booted high in the air, Davies arrived at just the moment it was caught by Meads and, with a head of steam up, he launched himself into the tackle. 'I heard a cracking sound followed by the breath being thumped out of his body,' Davies said. 'He went off but came back on, bandaged, to finish the match.'

Meads, who was 34 at the time, would go on to play all four Tests against the Lions, but he was a shadow of his former self. The extent of his injury was a talking point throughout the series, as the Lions established their superiority with a victory in the first Test that set the tone for the rest of the tour. The Lions won in New Zealand for the first time, Meads would never play for the All Blacks again and his praise for the Lions' No8 was fulsome. 'He moved with quite startling speed and intelligence, an instinctive reaction,' Meads said of Davies. 'I've always said he was the one player who had the biggest impact on that 1971 series.'

Praise indeed. That gangly youth had clearly developed into an athlete capable of looking after himself against the toughest of opponents. The next Lions tour, three years later, was played on the harder grounds of South Africa and gave Davies greater scope to exhibit the attacking side of his game, the fluid running with ball in hand that had earned him the moniker 'Merv the Swerve'. It was also a tour on which his partnership with Gareth Edwards – the No8 at the base, the scrum half waiting behind, ready to attack – was taken to a whole new level, knitting the Lions' forwards and backs together so beautifully.

In the tour match against Orange Free State in Bloemfontein, the Lions scored a dramatic late try to preserve their unbeaten record, Davies picking up neatly as the scrum lurched forward, Edwards anticipating precisely the moment he would pass, drifting out towards the wing, then flipping a pass back over his head from which JJ Williams scored. In the first Test at Cape Town, Davies was instrumental in securing possession at the tail of the lineout for Edwards to kick a drop-goal. And in the second Test in Pretoria, one of the great Lions tries was scored. Phil Bennett jinked his way out of his own 22, then Davies helped link the move together through a swift interchange of passes with Willie John McBride before Edwards added further impetus and JJ Williams, again, scored in the left corner. It was this role, acting as a conduit between backs and forwards, that Davies played so well.

Once again, though, against the ultra-aggressive Springboks, it would be the physical battle that determined the series, and once again Davies made a telling impact. This time it came in the first Test, when Boland Coetzee, the flanker who was reckoned to be one of the toughest Springboks, took an inside pass from his winger. Standing in front of him, Davies had anticipated the pass and launched himself horizontally at Coetzee. 'Merv cut him in half with that tackle and you could hear the crowd gasp,' Fran Cotton, the Lions prop, said. It showed that the Lions were not there to be pushed around, and they conclusively won the first Test, on the way to a historic series win.

'It was the tackle of my career and it gave me terrific pleasure,' Davies said. 'You can keep your fifty-yard runs and your wizard little sidesteps. For me, catching Coetzee right under his ribs, digging in hard and sending him wheezing 10 yards backwards onto his arse was bliss.'

Davies leads Wales out as captain before the Test against Australia in Cardiff in 1975

For the next two years, Davies was captain of Wales, leading them to the Five Nations title in 1975 and then another grand slam in 1976. He was widely expected to be asked to lead the Lions on their tour to New Zealand the following year. But 22 days after the grand slam had been clinched with victory over France in Cardiff, he was playing in a cup semi-final for Swansea against Pontypool when he collapsed on the field. He had suffered a brain haemorrhage that would leave him fighting for his life. Although he went on to make a gradual recovery, that semi-final would prove, at the age of 29, to be his final game of rugby.

It brought to an end his run of 38 consecutive internationals for Wales, dating back to that hugely unexpected call-up when he thought he was just getting started in club rugby. His playing career might have been cut short, but Davies had achieved an enormous amount. And he had done so in his own distinctive style, reshaping the way No8s would play in future. 'He won the ball at the back of the lineout, steadied everything, always took possession forward,' said Ian McLauchlan, his Lions teammate. 'He was the perfect No8.'

Dickie Jeeps, whose tally of 13 caps for the Lions has still only been exceeded by Willie John McBride

REPLACEMENTS/
HONOURABLE MENTIONS

Any modern-day game of rugby features not just the starting 15, but also eight replacements waiting their turn on the bench, making up a matchday squad of 23. The eight replacements named below make up our matchday squad of Immortals, but they are also, by definition, the ones who missed out by the narrowest of margins from selection in the starting line-up, pipped to the post by the great names in the preceding chapters. They are players who would feature as honourable mentions in any discussion of the greatest players in British and Irish rugby.

Some of the men chosen here actually played in a time before replacements were permitted. Before 1968, if there were injuries that forced a player from the field, their team had to soldier on with 14 men. Indeed, the first 'substitute' in international rugby was for the British & Irish Lions, when Mike Gibson replaced the injured Barry John during the

first Test against South Africa in Pretoria. By happy coincidence, Gibson is included among the selection of replacements here, while John is in my starting line-up, so that historical first could be repeated in our hypothetical game.

The replacements bench is configured along the lines generally used in the modern game, five forwards and three backs. So we have one hooker and two props, a second-row forward and a versatile back-rower, along with a scrum half, midfield back (capable of covering fly half and centre) and a back-three player who can fill in at full back or on the wing. The selection criteria are the same as for the starting 15, namely that they must have excelled for the British & Irish Lions and been on at least two tours. They will, no doubt, all feel they have a point to prove when they step into action, determined to demonstrate that they should not have been left out of the Immortals starting 15 in the first place.

Bobby Windsor gets to grips with Jean-Pierre Rives during Wales' victory over France in the 1978 Five Nations

No16 (hooker)
Bobby Windsor (Wales)

A member of the fabled Pontypool front row of the 1970s, Windsor was just the sort of character the Lions needed for their tour of South Africa in 1974. When Willie John McBride, the captain, told his touring squad before departure that they should expect all manner of physical intimidation and skulduggery from their opponents throughout the tour, and that anyone who did not relish the prospect would be welcome to leave, Windsor famously piped up: 'I'm going to bloody well love this!' He

went on to play an integral role in the series, packing down between Ian McLauchlan and Fran Cotton in all four Tests in what is generally considered to be the finest of all Lions forward packs. He also toured New Zealand in 1977.

Two England hookers could push Windsor close. Brian Moore was a charismatic presence in the dominant England pack of the late 1980s and early 1990s, several of whom were central to the Lions' series victory in Australia in 1989 and the tour to New Zealand in 1993, with Moore at the heart. Peter Wheeler picked up from Windsor

Tom Smith, centre, flanked by (left to right) Keith Wood, Tim Rodber, Lawrence Dallaglio and Martin Johnson before the second Test against South Africa in 1997

on the 1977 tour in New Zealand, where the Lions front row was so impressive, and helped to push the Springboks close in 1980, winning seven Lions Test caps in all.

No17 (loosehead prop) Tom Smith (Scotland)

For the role he played in South Africa in 1974, and his efforts in New Zealand three years earlier, 'Mighty Mouse' McLauchlan was a clear front-runner to start in the Immortals No1 shirt, but his fellow Scot, Tom Smith, was not far behind. The contribution of the front row to the Lions' success in South

Africa in 1997 was immense and the triumvirate of Smith, Keith Wood and Paul Wallace were a classic example of how Lions magic can work. Against a mighty South African pack, they were unfancied at the start of the series, and Wallace had only been called up because of injury to Peter Clohessy, his Ireland teammate. But they gelled as a front-row unit, despite never having played together as a unit before, and Smith was outstanding. Four years later, he started all three Tests in the near-miss against Australia.

Mako Vunipola, of England, was close to winning a place on the

England prop Fran Cotton started all four Tests for the Lions in South Africa in 1974

bench. With his all-court game, he was a potent impact replacement in Australia in 2013, started all three Tests in New Zealand in 2017, and then featured in all three matches against South Africa in 2021. Only one prop – Graham Price – has won more than Vunipola's nine Test caps for the Lions and his handling and carrying make him an excellent

player to have coming on from the bench against tiring opponents. But Smith's superior scrummaging and durability, which were such a force in that 1997 series, win him the nod.

No18 (tight-head prop) Fran Cotton (England)

When a front row gains the upper hand in a Test series, it makes sense for them to stay together, and that was the case in South Africa in 1974. In the most confrontational of series, McLauchlan, Windsor and Cotton went toe-to-toe with the Springboks front row as the Lions remained invincible throughout. Cotton could play on either side of the scrum, but this slab of solid scrummaging muscle played at tight-head in that series and was part of a monumental forward effort. 'Frannie was massive on that tour,' Windsor said. 'Like a great English oak.' To demonstrate his versatility, he played on the other side of the scrum in New Zealand three years later in another redoubtable front row, alongside Peter Wheeler and Graham Price.

Tadhg Furlong was chosen as the starting tight-head in our Immortals line-up because of the wide array of skills he brings in addition to set-piece solidity, but the Lions have been blessed with a number of powerful scrummaging tight-heads. Adam Jones was excellent in the 2013 series victory over Australia after being cruelly forced out of the 2009 series in South Africa by a dangerous clearout from Bakkies Botha. Graham Price, another one of the famous Pontypool front row, can count himself unfortunate to have played throughout three Test series – New Zealand in 1977 and 1983, South Africa in 1980 – and only won two matches, but his tally of 12 Test caps is a record for a Lions prop. A special mention, too, for Syd Millar, another who was comfortable on both sides of the scrum, who was a rock for the Lions in difficult times from 1958 to 1968, and played a major role in the 1974 success as forwards coach.

No19 (second row)
Alun Wyn Jones (Wales)

There were more potential Immortals in the second row than in perhaps any other position. The two starting locks, Willie John McBride and Maro Itoje, give a satisfying balance of power and skill, but there are several who missed out narrowly. It will be seen as sacrilegious by some to have left out Martin Johnson, inspirational

Alun Wyn Jones, during the 2021 series in South Africa, when he was made captain on his fourth Lions tour

captain on the tours to South Africa in 1997 and Australia in 2001. Paul O'Connell was one of the few to emerge from the disastrous tour to New Zealand in 2005 with his reputation enhanced, he was then colossal as captain on the tour to South Africa in 2009 and would have played a full part in the series win in

Australia four years later had injury not intervened after the first Test. Further back, Gordon Brown – the renowned 'Broon frae Troon' – was a thunderous presence in those epic series wins over the All Blacks in 1971 and the Springboks in 1974.

But Alun Wyn Jones wins his place on the Immortals bench through his longevity and success with the Lions. Starting alongside O'Connell in 2009, through to South Africa again in 2021, he played in 12 consecutive Lions Tests, including nine successive starts from 2013 to 2021. He captained the Lions in the decisive Test victory over Australia in 2013, formed a world-class second-row pairing with Itoje in 2017, then led throughout the series against the Springboks in 2021. With Wales, he won a record 158 caps. To play with such intensity and skill over such a sustained period, in such a physically demanding position, shows a player of rare gifts.

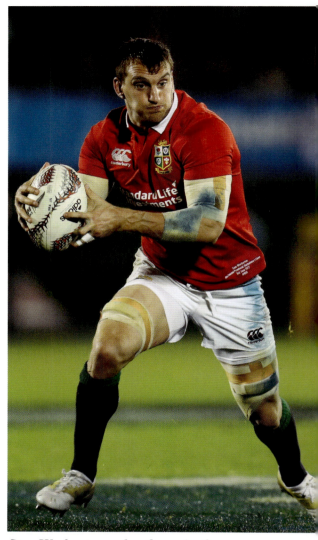

Sam Warburton, a key figure in the Lions' tours to Australia in 2013 and New Zealand four years later

No20 (back row)
Sam Warburton (Wales)

Any number of back-row players could have taken this spot on the bench. While Richard Hill and Seán O'Brien emerged from a crowded field to start as flankers in the Immortals starting line-up, John Taylor and Fergus Slattery came close for their roles in the Lions' triumphs of the early 1970s. Lawrence Dallaglio, known principally as a No8, was outstanding as blindside flanker on the successful tour to South Africa in

Scrum half Dickie Jeeps, who was uncapped by England before the 1955 Lions tour to South Africa, yet started all four Tests

came from nowhere to play a key role in South Africa in 2009.

This bench position could also have gone to a specialist No8. Although Mervyn Davies was a clear front-runner for the starting line-up, there are others in his position who have excelled: Dean Richards in 1989 and 1993, Jamie Heaslip in 2009 and 2013, and Taulupe Faletau, who was very close to securing this spot on the bench, in the decisive third Test in Australia in 2013 and throughout the 2017 series against the All Blacks.

But Sam Warburton was a central figure in two successful tours. He was the youngest Lions captain, aged 24, when chosen to lead the tour to Australia in 2013, and started the first two Tests at No7 before missing the third through injury. He was captain again in New Zealand four years later, and played No6 in a harmonious pairing with O'Brien. As he demonstrated in those two series, Warburton can cover both blindside and openside positions, always useful in a replacement.

No21 (scrum half)
Dickie Jeeps (England)

One of the joys of British & Irish Lions tours is the emergence of unexpected heroes, unfancied when

1997, forming a dynamic all-English back row with Richard Hill and Tim Rodber that helped to secure the series, although his two subsequent tours with the Lions were ruined by injury. Tom Croft, despite not being chosen in the original squad,

the plane leaves home, but taking their chance with both hands once they arrive. Dickie Jeeps was one such case, uncapped by England when he went to South Africa with the Lions in 1955, and considered the third-choice scrum half, but he ended up starting all four Tests. Alongside Cliff Morgan, of Wales, he formed an effective half-back pairing as the Lions earned a highly creditable 2–2 draw in the series. More than that, he then went on two more Lions tours and won 13 Test caps in all, a tally exceeded only by Willie John McBride. Jeeps provided a reliable service to his fly halves and, nicknamed the 'India Rubber Man' on tour to New Zealand, he was unflappable in the face of personal attention from marauding opposition back rows, a vital quality on tours of the southern hemisphere.

The same could be said for Mike Phillips, the Wales scrum half, who was a crucial cog in the tours of South Africa in 2009 and Australia four years later. Built more like a flanker than a scrum half, Phillips was a highly robust No9, but still capable of making darting breaks around the fringes. Matt Dawson enjoyed a fine series in South Africa in 1997, including

his famous dummy for a try in the first Test, and Robert Jones contributed so much towards the series win in Australia in 1989.

No22 (inside back) Mike Gibson (Ireland)

The versatility that Gibson would bring to the bench is illustrated by his record of playing fly half during the 1968 Lions tour to South Africa, having come on to replace Barry John in that first Test, after playing inside centre in New Zealand in 1966 and then going on to play outside centre against the All Blacks in 1971. Gibson, no doubt, was one of the all-time greats, highly intelligent with ball in hand and a smart defender, and he missed out by a whisker on a place in the starting line-up to Jeremy Guscott at No13, which was perhaps his best position. He went on five Lions tours in total, joining the 1974 trip late through work commitments, and was then prevented from competing for a place in the Test team in 1977 due to injury.

Choosing Gibson means that there will not be a second out-and-out fly half. That means that Phil Bennett, who was so wonderful in South Africa in 1974, has been

Mike Gibson (right), with Gordon Brown and Bob Hiller at Heathrow Airport before the Lions' 1971 tour to New Zealand

squeezed out, while Johnny Sexton, a more recent playmaking maestro, is also surplus to requirements.

Among the centres, Brian O'Driscoll was another who missed out narrowly to Guscott, and he misses out on the bench because of Gibson's ability to cover different positions. Shades, perhaps, of Warren Gatland's controversial decision to omit O'Driscoll from the deciding Test against the Wallabies in 2013?

Two Welsh centres are particularly unfortunate to miss out on a place in the matchday squad: Scott Gibbs, who was such a force at inside centre alongside Guscott in 1993 and 1997, and Jonathan Davies. Capable of filling either centre position, Davies had two Tests at No12 and one at

Andy Irvine of Scotland excelled both on the wing and at full back for the Lions

No13 in 2013, then all three Tests at outside centre in New Zealand in 2017, when he was man of the series. But Guscott's magic Lions moments have taken precedence.

No23 (wing/full back) Andy Irvine (Scotland)

As we're looking for an outside back who can cover both wing and full back, Andy Irvine fits the bill perfectly. For the Lions against the Springboks in 1974, he came into the side for the last two Tests on the wing and played a crucial role, including some outstanding goal-kicking. He then played his preferred position of full back for all four Tests against the All Blacks in 1977 and for three of the four Tests back in South Africa three years later.

If we had just been looking for full back cover, then his fellow Scot, Gavin Hastings, would have had a compelling case, as a rock at the back during the successful 1989 tour of Australia and then captain in New Zealand in 1993. But Irvine's stint on the wing in South Africa earns him the vote. Leigh Halfpenny was another full back under consideration, especially as he played on the wing for Wales as well, after his man-of-the-series heroics against the Wallabies in 2013, not

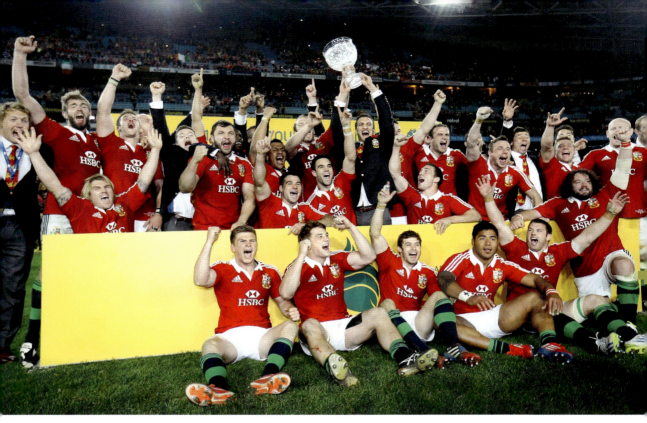

The 2013 Lions celebrate their series victory over Australia, clinched with a thumping win in the decisive third Test in Sydney

just his prolific goal-kicking, but his brilliant performance in the final Test in Sydney. But he did not start another Test for the Lions, missing out with injury in 2009 and coming off the bench once against the All Blacks in 2017.

A number of wingers could have been contenders. Tony O'Reilly, of Ireland, was brilliant for the Lions in South Africa in 1955 and New Zealand and Australia four years later. His tally of six Test tries remains a Lions record and he went on to become a highly successful businessman, as chief executive of Heinz, among other things. Ieuan Evans was another who served the

Lions superbly, playing his part in three series, but memorably crowning the Lions' fightback from 1–0 down against Australia in 1989 by scoring the series-clinching try in the deciding Test.

BIBLIOGRAPHY

BOOKS

Bennett, Phil, *The Autobiography*, CollinsWillow, 2003.

Dallaglio, Lawrence, *It's in the Blood: My Life*, Headline, 2008

Dallaglio, Lawrence & Slot, Owen, *The Boys of Winter*, Blink, 2023

Davies, Gerald, *An Autobiography*, Allen & Unwin, 1979

Davies, Mervyn & Roach, David, *In Strength and Shadow*, Mainstream, 2005

English, Tom & Burns, Peter, *This is Your Everest*, Polaris, 2021

Hill, Richard, *The Autobiography*, Orion, 2007

Jones, Stephen et al., *Behind the Lions*, Polaris, 2012

McGeechan, Ian, *The Lions: When the Going Gets Tough*, Hodder & Stoughton, 2017

Roberts, Jamie, *Centre Stage*, Hodder & Stoughton, 2021

Thomas, Clem & Greg, *125 Years of the British & Irish Lions*, Mainstream, 2013

Williams, JJ, *The Life and Times of a Rugby Legend*, Y Lolfa, 2015

Williams, JPR, *Given the Breaks, My Life in Rugby*, Hodder & Stoughton, 2006

NEWSPAPERS

Belfast Telegraph
Daily Telegraph
The Guardian
The Herald
Irish Examiner
The Scotsman
The Times
The Sunday Times

TELEVISION

Willie John, BBC Northern Ireland, 2015
Living with Lions, 1999

INTERNET

espnscrum.com
lionsrugby.com
YouTube.com
en.wikipedia.org
walesonline.co.uk

ACKNOWLEDGEMENTS

Huge thanks to Melanie Michael-Greer for her work in getting this project off the ground. To Luke West, Katie Stackhouse, Brooke Halliwell and the rest of the team at Rockpool Publishing, thanks for your professional and skilful approach in bringing the book to life. And to everyone involved with keeping the British & Irish Lions show on the road, the game of rugby owes an unstinting gratitude. I hope this book offers another reminder that the memories created on those tours, in those special quadrennial contests, are like nothing else in the sporting world.

ABOUT THE AUTHOR

John Westerby has been a sports writer for *The Times* since 2003. He has worked on World Cups in rugby union, cricket and rugby league, British & Irish Lions tours and Ashes series, as well as Premier League football, the Olympics and Paralympic Games, the Ryder Cup and Open Championships in golf, cycling World Championships on track and road, and grand slam tennis championships.

He was the co-author of *Hoggy*, Matthew Hoggard's autobiography, has written for Wisden Cricketers' Almanack and contributed to *England's World Cup: The full story of the 2019 tournament*.

He grew up in Mirfield, West Yorkshire, playing and watching rugby, cricket, football and any other sport he could find. He now lives on the wrong side of the Roses divide near Manchester with his wife, Sally, and their children, Will, Sam and Alice, and enjoys watching their sporting exploits from the sidelines without having to file a match report immediately afterwards.

ALSO IN THE SERIES

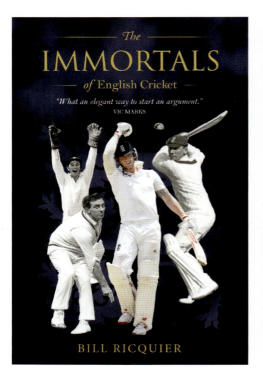

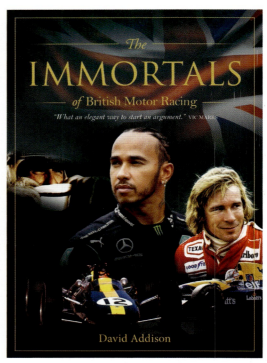

Immortals of English Cricket
by Bill Ricquier
ISBN: 9781925946123

Immortals of British Motor Racing
by David Addison
ISBN: 9781922662019

Available now from all good book stores.
geldingstreetpress.com